The PathFinder

A Guide to Career Decision Making

REVISED EDITION

LEE ELLIS

Foreword by Larry Burkett

An Outreach Ministry of Christian Financial Concepts, Inc.

About Career Pathways . . .

Career Pathways is the career guidance outreach of Christian Financial Concepts (CFC) of Gainesville, Georgia. Since 1976, under the leadership of Larry Burkett, CFC has focused its ministry on teaching biblical principles of handling money. Career Pathways expands CFC's emphasis on stewardship to include stewardship of other talents, i.e., our unique gifts, abilities, and personal styles of work.

Based on the biblical teaching that God has a purpose for each individual, the Career Pathways program seeks to reaffirm the Christian perspective by revealing how our work is really a part of fulfilling God's purpose.

Career Pathways seeks to help individuals discover their talents and career direction by providing education, testing, and feedback. More than 16,000 people, ages 16 to 72, have received individualized assessments through the Career Pathways program.

About the Author . . .

Lee Ellis served as a career Air Force officer until his retirement in 1989. During the Vietnam war, his aircraft was shot down and he was a prisoner of war for over five years.

During Lee's military career, his assignments included duty as a pilot, flight instructor, staff officer, flying squadron commander, and supervisor in higher education.

In addition to earning a Bachelor of Arts degree in history from the University of Georgia and a Master of Science degree in counseling and human development from Troy State University, Lee is a graduate of the Armed Forces Staff College and the Air War College.

While in the Air Force Lee became a volunteer teacher and counselor for Christian Financial Concepts. He believes that God has a special purpose for each person. During his 17 years of supervising, educating, and training young people, he saw clearly how God has gifted people with different talents for service in the Kingdom.

In January 1990, Lee became the director of Career Pathways. He has since co-authored two books with Larry Burkett, *Your Career in Changing Times* and *Finding the Career That Fits You*. Under his leadership from 1990 to 1995, Career Pathways has researched and produced numerous career-related testing instruments.

Revised Edition - 1995

Printed in the U.S.A.

ISBN
1-56427-080-7

Contents

Continued

Contents (continued)

Foreword

During the years I was counseling families on their finances, I frequently observed people in career fields that didn't match their talents and abilities. It concerned me that so many people were not aware of their strengths and, therefore, were not being good stewards of their talents.

I began to pray that someone would develop a program that would help people understand their vocational bent and show them how to make the right career decisions. In 1989 I felt the Lord was leading Christian Financial Concepts to undertake this task. Lee Ellis, one of our lay counselors, was retiring from the Air Force about that time, and so I challenged him to come to CFC and develop the program that is now Career Pathways.

The PathFinder is a tool for individuals and families who are making career decisions. It begins by focusing on a biblical perspective of work: **Our work is unto the Lord and for His glory.** The manual provides a wealth of information and offers many resources for making career and life decisions. It provides practical steps for choosing the right career field and also gives instructions for getting a job.

I know Lee Ellis and his team have developed *The PathFinder* to answer many of the questions posed by those in career transition. You will find sound career counsel from a biblical perspective throughout the manual. Since it has been designed as a broad resource, you may not use every chapter immediately.

I believe *The PathFinder* will be invaluable to you and your family as you seek God's plan for your lives.

In Christ,

Larry

Larry Burkett

Introduction

In this day of one-hour photo finishing, two-minute car washes, and instant breakfasts, often we are led to think that there is a quick fix for most of life's challenges. Unfortunately, there are generally no quick, easy answers as to which way to go at the many crossroads of life.

Sooner or later we learn by experience that it takes time, effort, and commitment to resolve the issues that arise in the journey of life. Viewed in the larger sense, becoming Christ-like is a process of living one day at a time, "renewing our minds" in Him. Ultimately, most of the important things in life are viewed best as a process rather than an event. Career decision making is certainly one of those areas that is not an event but a process.

Many of the readers of this manual will have had the Career Pathways assessment. The assessment tells you a lot about your pattern for work and, with your follow-up, it will give you a very good description of the type of work for which you are best suited. The assessment provides good general information and offers alternatives for consideration, but neither the reports nor Career Pathways can tell a person exactly what to do.

Counselors are taught not to make decisions for the client, even though that is often what the client wants. Ultimately, the individual has to evaluate the options and make decisions. This PathFinder will help you in that process. Most of the material is foundational and will serve you well as you move through the various stages of your career.

We can't stress enough the following formula for success. Pray for guidance, work the process, and trust God for the results. If you will follow these three steps, we are confident you will end up in a situation in which God blesses you with a career pathway that will honor Him.

"I am the light of the world.
Whoever follows me will never walk in darkness,
but will have the light of life" (John 8:12).

1 Looking at Work from a Biblical Perspective

Why Are So Many People Unhappy in Their Work?

Job dissatisfaction is almost the norm today, and at Career Pathways we hear about many of the problems in the workplace. The primary cause of discontentment, we have concluded, is that we have lost the biblical perspective of work.

Somehow we, as a society, have adopted a "secular" view of work—a view that allows us to think we can separate our work from our spiritual lives.

This heresy in our thinking has led to most of the misery we see now in the workplace. As in other areas of our lives, when we operate with unsound concepts, we suffer the consequences.

In our early days as a nation, even those who were not devout Christians had a concept of a divine calling in their work. In general, work was seen in a more honorable light—as a way to fulfill one's purpose in life.

Although at one time work may have been considered a calling, it now seems to be merely a means to an end. Work allows us to purchase pleasure, to fulfill our materialistic needs, and to build our egos by gaining power and position. This misguided view of what work is all about has led us to the point at which 60 to 80 percent of those in the work force are dissatisfied with their jobs.

It would be good to begin the career-decision process by taking a look at the errors and the truths that relate to work. If operating under false beliefs is causing so much stress and heartache, then the truth should set us free to find the joy in work that our Creator intended.

Let's look first at some of the errors and the problems they cause.

MATERIALISM (GREED)

"What good is it for a man to gain the whole world, and yet lose or forfeit his very self?" (Luke 9:25).

Probably the biggest deception regarding work in our society today is the belief that a higher income (more money) can bring happiness. Most Career Pathways clients are adults who have jobs and are making "adequate" money, yet they are not fulfilled. Many of them say without hesitation that they pursued their present careers because those careers offered prestige and high incomes. Now they see the mistake in making decisions based primarily on income. Money does not provide satisfaction.

We hear movie stars, athletes, and other high income celebrities say the same thing. In an interview with *World Wide Challenge* (Campus Crusade for Christ) magazine, Christopher Parkening, one of the preeminent virtuosos of the classical guitar, said it well:

"Keep your lives free from the love of money and be content with what you have, because God has said 'Never will I leave you; Never will I forsake you'" (Hebrews 13:5).

> "The world tells you that success is having a lot of money, being famous and being independent —doing what you want to do, when you want to do it. For years I pursued success in the music field to the point that I was able to retire to a Montana ranch at age 30. My wife and I were living what most would consider the ideal life. But a year after I got everything I wanted, it meant absolutely nothing. I was empty inside.
>
> "During that period of time I became a Christian, and my priorities changed. When I came across the passage in 1 Corinthians that says, 'Whatever you do, do all for the glory of God,' I realized there were only two things I knew how to do. One was fly fish and the other was play the guitar.
>
> "I went back to playing the guitar, but this time with a different purpose. As Bach once said, 'The aim and final reason of all music is none else but the glory of God.' "

PRIDE

A second problem is pride. We are so concerned with what the world might think or say if we happened to get into something that is not a "successful" job or a "good position," we are ashamed to do what God has created us to do. We then burn ourselves out trying to do jobs we were not naturally designed to do. You can call it going against the grain, not following your bent, or swimming upstream, but the bottom line is that it's impossible to be excellent for very long when you're not using the talents and strengths God has given you (see Psalm 139:13).

"Pride goes before destruction, a haughty spirit before a fall. Better to be lowly in spirit and among the oppressed than to share plunder with the proud" (Proverbs 16:18-19).

Many of our clients are in the wrong jobs because of their parents' pride. As young people, they were pushed into career fields so they could "be somebody" or "amount to something." To put it plainly, we parents often want to fulfill our own worldly dreams and boost our egos through our children.

Jesus tried to point out to the Pharisees that they were concerned with impressing men with their outward appearances (or reputations). But Jesus was concerned with what was inside—the motivation of the heart (or character). You will recall that was His main problem with the Pharisees. He called them hypocrites because they cleaned the outside of the cup and dish but inside they were full of greed and self-indulgence. He wanted them to clean the inside of the cup and dish (motivation to serve others), and then the outside also would be clean (see Matthew 23:25-26). The Lord made this concept clear to Samuel when He chose to anoint David rather than one of his more handsome brothers. He reminded Samuel that the Lord looks at the heart.

"The Lord does not look at the things man looks at. Man looks at the outward appearance, but the Lord looks at the heart" (1 Samuel 16:7).

LACK OF TRUST (FAITH)

A third problem that gets us off course in our pursuit of a rewarding career pathway is a lack of real faith; or, said another way: Deep down we really don't trust that God is sufficient for all our needs. We are driven to "achieve success" so we can eventually gain control of our circumstances and be independent (protected) from the problems of life. This really reflects a fundamental error in our thinking. There is no security in this world. Achievement, more independence, and control will not help.

Witness the high-ranking executives and famous people who become alcoholics or commit suicide each year. There are no guarantees in this life aside from the promises of God's Word, which have been sealed through the unconditional love of Christ and the gift of His Holy Spirit. We must walk each day in faith—depending on Him for every breath.

"I am the vine; you are the branches. If a man remains in me and I in him, he will bear much fruit; ***apart from me you can do nothing"*** (John 15:5, emphasis added).

The apostle Paul goes to great lengths to point out the role of faith: ***"And without faith it is impossible to please God,*** *because anyone who comes to him must believe that he exists and that he rewards those who earnestly seek him"* (Hebrews 11:6, emphasis added).

The problem is that most of us don't really trust God to be involved personally in our lives, and we miss out on His perfect plan.

So if we are not able to control the future through achievement, we have two options: wrap ourselves in a cloak of despair, or trust in a personal God who loves us and wants His very best for us. The choice is clear, but it can only be made in faith, and that means returning control of your life to the Author of Life (see Matthew 6:33-34).

"The simple inherit folly, but the prudent are crowned with knowledge" (Proverbs 14:18).

IGNORANCE

A final reason for poor career decisions is ignorance. Many of our clients took available jobs just because they never had been taught how to make career decisions. Virtually no one in our society has offered a sound plan for teaching people how to make career choices. Sure, there are a few good books on the subject, but there is a pitiful silence from institutions such as churches, schools, and government. Our experience has been that even most Christians have adopted the world's values about work (materialism, pride, control). Our prayer is that Christians will recognize that a self-centered, materialistic career orientation does not work. It should be clear that any program of career guidance must be built on a solid foundation—a foundation of truth (see 1 Corinthians 3:10-15).

What Are Some Truths About Work?

"If you hold to My teaching, you are really My disciples. Then you will know the truth, and the truth will set you free" (John 8:31-32).

GOD WORKS

Chapter one of Genesis documents God's work in creating the universe. Furthermore, the entire Bible documents God's work as Lord and Ruler of the universe. We see His work as he protected His people from the Pharaoh on their journey out of Egypt. We see His work as He looked after one individual like David, and He tells us that He has numbered even the hairs on our heads. God is obviously not neglecting His work of being God.

Christ was directly involved in the creation and, though fully God, He became fully man and worked on this earth. Apparently Jesus was involved in common labor and, even in the height of his ministry, he was never employed by the church of his day. Finally, Jesus carried out his most significant work as a Suffering Servant—at the cross, obeying the will of the Father.

"The Lord God took the man and put him in the Garden of Eden to work it and take care of it" (Genesis 2:15).

GOD COMMISSIONED WORK

If we are created in God's image, then we also are divinely ordained for work. Genesis 1:26-30 details our role in work: we rule over the lower creation. We were commissioned to work even before the fall. To be sure, after the original sin the nature of work became more difficult. Furthermore, work and the product of it could be used for good or evil. Yet the clear implication throughout the Bible is that work is part of the divine nature and, therefore, should bring glory to our Creator.

We are to use the talents God has given us and, in doing so, glorify Him.

It honors the Father when we are true to our creation. Ralph Mattson and Arthur Miller make this point quite well in their book, *Finding a Job You Can Love* (Thomas Nelson Publishers).

> "We please God when we act the way we are designed to act, when we are who God designed us to be. When such actions are carried out with the intention of being expressions of love to Him, they do in fact become expressions of love to Him."

Let me illustrate what it means to be what God designed you to be. As a young man, one of our clients wanted to be a youth leader and work in the area of recreation or at the YMCA. Instead, he became a computer programmer because his parents told him he needed to make more money and be more "successful." When he came to us he was in his late twenties and had burned out on his "successful" job. His career assessment clearly revealed how God had equipped him to be an encourager and leader of youth.

We can report happily that this client is now in the process of becoming a YMCA leader and his life has taken on new meaning. He is excited because he is getting to do what he was designed to do. Can you imagine a bluebird trying to be a woodpecker just so it can attract more attention? His bill is not equipped for drilling holes. A bluebird honors its creator by being a very beautiful bluebird. Likewise, those who recognize their talents and use them to the glory of the Lord become a magnificent testimony to the work of the Creator.

"There are different kinds of service, but the same Lord"
(1 Corinthians 12:5).

In their book, *Your Work Matters to God* (Navpress), Doug Sherman and Bill Hendricks provide an in-depth look at the biblical view of work. They point out that the workplace is a primary place for our witness; and the income from our work is used to honor God through giving our tithe, providing for our families, and generating a surplus with which to help others. If you thought that ministry was only for full-time professionals, you definitely should read the works of Sherman and Hendricks.

A MOTHER'S PRIMARY CALLING IS TO NURTURE HER YOUNG

Everyone does not have to earn a paycheck to fulfill his or her calling. Mothers are called to bear and nurture children, and this responsibility must come before career. With all the talk about choosing a career and a social climate driven by materialism, it may seem natural for mothers to believe they have to have a career in order to be fulfilled. But remember, fulfillment comes from knowing we are in God's will by carrying out His purpose for our lives.

Scripture does not preclude women being employed outside the home, but it does indicate that there are higher responsibilities which may preclude a "normal" career while the children are young.

Generally, women have been gifted much better than men to be the nurturers of the home and family. We believe that many of the problems of our society today are a direct result of parents becoming overly committed with work and leisure, at the expense of the nurturing of their children.

The focal point for love and quality instruction to children in the home is the mother. As such, her role is the most important one in our society. If she fails, society fails. Of course, the sacrificial love and support of the husband is an essential element of what she needs to do her job.

Experience shows that a Career Pathways assessment is valuable for every woman. If she is a mother and homemaker, she will be able to do her job better if she knows her pattern of strengths and weaknesses. An assessment will help her choose an educational and training track which highlights her strengths. If she decides to pursue a career, she will know how to make good vocational choices.

Our work provides an opportunity to carry out the Great Commission.

WE ARE TO BE BLESSINGS TO OTHERS

We can trace this commission to the Old Testament and God's covenant with Abram in Genesis 12:2-3 where He says, *"I will bless you . . . and all peoples on earth will be blessed through you."* We are descendants of Abram and we are the branches through which flow the blessings—the "rivers of water" which yield eternal life.

WE ARE TO BE LIGHTS TO THE WORLD

Once we have encountered Jesus Christ, we are to be different. He is in us and produces the light that attracts others to Him. *"In Him was life, and that life was the light of men"* (John 1:4).

"In the same way, let your light shine before men, ***that they may see your good deeds and praise your Father in heaven"*** (Matthew 5:16, emphasis added).

He told us, *"You are the light of the world. A city on a hill cannot be hidden. Neither do people light a lamp and put it under a bowl. Instead they put it on its stand, and it gives light to everyone in the house"* (Matthew 5:14-15).

The apostle Paul again defines the role of light in Acts 13:47: *"For this is what the Lord has commanded us: 'I have made you a light for the Gentiles, that you may bring salvation to the ends of the earth.'"* By taking the presence of Jesus into the work place, we bear the light that truly is "a blessing to all peoples."

In our work we are to be vessels of the light, showing the way through the Son to the Father. What a great mission! But how can we be attractive to anyone if we are motivated by greed, pride, a futile drive for independence, or ignorance? We can't!

We must remember that we have a special mission; it is sacred and, therefore, we cannot escape the conclusion that our work must be unto the Lord. Ultimately, our attitudes and performance at work will either honor Him or detract from Him.

Perhaps you have made some career mistakes due to errors in thinking. If so, you can be like the apostle Paul: Forget what is behind and strain toward what is ahead; press on toward the goal to win the prize for which God has called you heavenward in Christ Jesus (see Philippians 3:13-14).

▶ *WE ARE TO LIVE BY TRUTH*

We pray that as you go through this manual, you will come face to face with your Creator and gain a new perspective on His truths regarding work. If you are like most of us, this will be a painful, yet liberating, experience. The pain comes from confronting our past sinful motivations, but we can take joy in knowing He forgives and does not remember our selfish past. By using our talents to be who we were created to be, we throw off the bondage of errors regarding work, and we are freed to serve as living testimonies. When our motivation is to be Christlike and to serve, our lights (reflections of Jesus, the source of all light) will not be hindered but will shine clearly for all to see.

"But whoever lives by the truth comes into the light, so that it may be seen plainly that what He has done has been done through God" (John 3:21).

The foundation for all career planning is the biblical principle that everything we do is unto the Lord.

Without a biblical view toward work, at best, our efforts can provide only temporary satisfaction for our egos. But our work can bring great joy when viewed from the perspective of the Christian's purpose on earth.

As we are able to trust the Lord in this important area of our lives, He increases our faith and reveals or confirms career pathways that will bring Him the glory, honor, and praise; and that's the best of all possible outcomes of our work. ◆

"Whether you eat or drink or whatever you do, do it all for the glory of God" (1 Corinthians 10:31).

BIBLICAL PRINCIPLES OF THE CAREER PLANNING PROCESS

1. We are unique creations of God.
"For you created my inmost being; you knit me together in my mother's womb. I praise you because I am fearfully and wonderfully made; your works are wonderful, I know that full well" (Psalm 139:13-14).

2. God blesses us individually with work-related talents.
"We have different gifts, according to the grace given us. If a man's gift is prophesying, let him use it in proportion to his faith. If it is serving, let him serve; if it is teaching, let him teach; if it is encouraging, let him encourage; if it is contributing to the needs of others, let him give generously; if it is leadership, let him govern diligently; if it is showing mercy, let him do it cheerfully" (Romans 12:6-8).

3. We are to be excellent in our work and examples to others. Excellence comes from development of our God-given talents.
"Do you see a man skilled in his work? He will serve before kings; he will not serve before obscure men" (Proverbs 22:29).

4. Our larger calling is to be witnesses for Christ and lights unto the world. This is greatly enhanced when we are experiencing the joy of using our talents at work.
"Let your light shine before men, that they may see your good deeds and praise your Father in heaven" (Matthew 5:16).

2 Understanding Your Pattern

To find your calling, you need to know something about the one being called—how God has gifted you for your calling.

Everywhere you turn today you hear about people who are searching to "find themselves." This search indicates that many are missing something in their lives. We believe that the missing ingredients can be found only by *discovering your Maker, understanding how He has made you,* and *acknowledging His mission for your life.* These issues define the who, why, and what that give meaning to life.

It is this search for a mission that usually brings someone to Career Pathways. In this chapter you will examine these issues from a broad perspective—looking specifically at how you can personally discover something about your *mission.*

As an overriding principle, we can say that your mission is shaped by the pattern of talents and interests you have been given.

"For you created my inmost being; you knit me together in my mother's womb. I praise you because I am fearfully and wonderfully made" (Psalm 139:13-14).

So if you understand "Your Pattern," you know a lot more about your mission in life.

In *What Color Is Your Parachute?* (Ten Speed Press), the best-selling book on career development, Richard Bolles has included a section entitled "How to Find Your Mission in Life." Bolles believes our missions are somewhat pre-set by our inborn pattern of talents and by the unique desires of our hearts.

The Career Pathways Assessment is designed to identify these two major areas: the **talents,** which include your abilities, skills, and personality strengths; and the **desires of your heart,** as expressed in vocational interests and work priorities. As you discover "Your Pattern" (see page 24), you'll see that you are indeed "knit together" in a tapestry that is purposefully and wonderfully made.

If you are aware of your pattern, and seek to employ it in an occupation that honors God, He will bless you and fill your need to "find yourself." You will then see how He is using you to be a blessing to others and a light to the world.

Your Pattern Has Four Major Components

Through research and experience, we have found four major identifiable parts to a pattern: these are skills and abilities, vocational interests, personality, and work priorities and values.

For the sake of discussion, let's use the analogy of concentric circles to explain the concept of a pattern.

As you can see, there is overlap between each area. In fact, we chose this concept to explain the pattern because each dimension is related to the others. Also, the concentric circles are smaller and more defining as you move toward the center. You can see that ultimately your values bring a narrow, but critical, focus to your pattern.

SKILLS AND ABILITIES

In the outer ring, which can be very broad, are **skills and abilities.** By the mere fact that we are human, each one of us has been given a broad range of abilities. For the most part, we all can communicate, use logic and reasoning, work with our hands, and carry out intellectual processes.

"Each one should use whatever gift he has received to serve others, faithfully administering God's grace in its various forms" (1 Peter 4:10).

When looking at your pattern, however, you need to focus on the abilities and processes that are easy for you. These are natural strengths that allow you to become highly skilled or to learn specialized processes more easily than most people of your age and experience.

Pay particular attention to the abilities you have used successfully and enjoyably. Remember your play activities as a youth, and think about the processes in which you excelled. Look at your hobbies now; it is likely they use some of your strengths.

In reviewing these highlights, probably you'll see the same environments and processes occurring over and over. Once identified, these same activities or processes should be transferred into your work environment. In their insightful book, *Finding a Job You Can Love* (Thomas Nelson Publishers), Christian authors Ralph Mattson and Arthur Miller describe in detail the significance of these recurring "motifs" in our lives' successes.

VOCATIONAL INTERESTS

Some job areas seem to appeal naturally to us, while others don't, and these desires of the heart are our vocational interests.

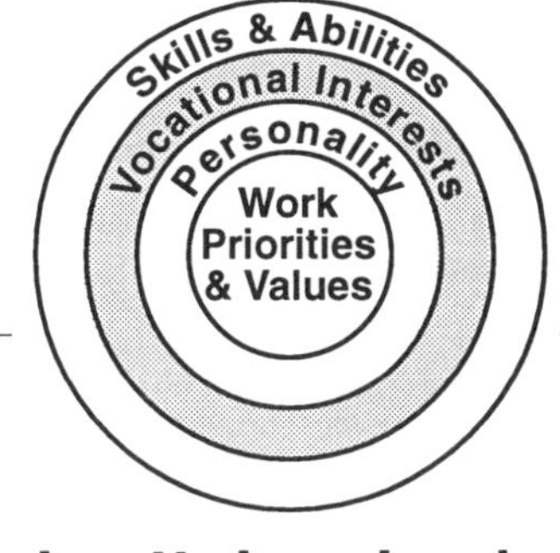

If we accept the concept that God gave us our patterns and our desires, it seems to follow that if we are committed to Him, then He has already written His will for us in our hearts.

"In his heart a man plans his course, but the Lord determines his steps" (Proverbs 16:9).

Our role then is to follow His will and apply it with wisdom under the guidance of the Holy Spirit.

Vocational interest inventories identify the desires of the heart. With over 30,000 occupations in the United States, inventories survey only a small number of them; however, your choices are generally representative of the occupational groups that most appeal to you. You should identify career fields that appeal to you and then look at a variety of occupations within those fields.

What Level of Job Is Best for You?

An additional issue to consider when appraising vocational interests is the level of job you want to pursue. You may want to pursue a highly skilled job or professional level job. The decision you will have to make is how much training and education are needed and how much you are willing to pursue.

In today's world the amount of knowledge is expanding at an increasing rate. There is a growing need for a skilled, highly trained, well-educated work force. We encourage you to get as much training and education as possible.

"His banner over me is love" (Song of Solomon 2:4).

PERSONALITY (TEMPERAMENT)

As you move from vocational interests into the area of personality, you gain a more refined insight into both your talents and the desires of your heart. Personality includes both abilities and interests but goes even further—into needs. Your personal profile reveals many of your core strengths and weaknesses and, for that reason, it provides important information about your behavioral pattern.

Each of us responds to people and situations in a certain way. In a group, some people want to talk while some prefer to listen. Likewise, some people need variety and adventure, while others need predictability and security.

You work most effectively when you use your own personal pattern of strengths.

Knowing and using your pattern will be especially important to your work and career success.

Listed below are the six factors of behavior measured by the Career Pathways Personality Inventory. Each factor is portrayed across a range of possible behaviors, as in ***dominant versus compliant.*** Each point on the range has strengths and weaknesses. This underscores that there is no "best" personality type. Regardless of how God has created you, you have strengths to take advantage of. Some people who have mixed tendencies will likely identify with some of both characteristics.

Summary Chart of Factors

		Mixed		
Compliant			◆	Dominant
Introverted			◆	Extroverted
Detached	◆			Compassionate
Unstructured	◆			Conscientious
Cautious			◆	Adventurous
Conventional		◆		Innovative

The person in the chart above is dominant, extroverted, detached, unstructured, adventurous, and mixed in terms of innovative abilities. Specific characteristics of these factors are listed on next page.

DOMINANT

STRENGTHS

- Leadership oriented; likes to control the process and outcome.
- Influential; presses hard to reach goals and ideas.
- Bold in adversity; direct and straightforward.

WEAKNESSES

- Can be pushy in order to get results.
- Forgets that success is usually a team effort.
- Insensitive to feelings of others.

vs

COMPLIANT

STRENGTHS

- Diplomatic with others.
- Good team player, cooperative.
- Servant's attitude, desires to help in practical ways.

WEAKNESSES

- May withhold true feelings.
- Not assertive.
- Underestimates self.

EXTROVERTED

STRENGTHS

- Upbeat, positive outlook.
- Energetic, enthusiastic.
- Good networker, social.
- Persuasive, motivational.

WEAKNESSES

- Overly optimistic.
- Becomes overcommitted.
- Poor time management.
- Gets distracted from the task.

vs

INTROVERTED

STRENGTHS

- Relies on logic rather than emotion.
- Works well independently.
- Thoughtful listener, succinct in speech.

WEAKNESSES

- Low energy level.
- May appear aloof, unfriendly.
- Stressed by social events.
- Dull public speaker.

COMPASSIONATE

STRENGTHS

- Compassionate, sensitive to the needs of others.
- Good at encouraging others.
- Agreeable, cooperative.
- Good listener.
- Warm-hearted, caring.
- Tolerant of others' mistakes.

WEAKNESSES

- Naive, easily manipulated.
- Difficulty in saying "no."
- Stressed by conflict; avoids confrontation.
- Neglects personal needs to care for others, and may become resentful.

vs

DETACHED

STRENGTHS

- Strong task orientation; not deterred by criticism.
- Confronts others easily.
- Tough negotiator, good at bargaining.

WEAKNESSES

- Comes across as cold or uncaring.
- Overlooks appropriate expressions of mercy.
- Impatient with others.

CONSCIENTIOUS

STRENGTHS

- Very good with details.
- Thorough and precise.
- Highly organized.
- Good, efficient planner.

WEAKNESSES

- May hold unreasonably high expectations of self, others.
- Overly cautious.
- Rigid, inflexible, legalistic.

vs

UNSTRUCTURED

STRENGTHS

- Ability to see "big picture."
- Excels at improvising.
- Independent, free-spirited.
- Very flexible, spontaneous.

WEAKNESSES

- Tendency toward disorganization.
- Overlooks important facts.
- Unprepared, "wings it."
- Has a problem completing what is started.

ADVENTUROUS

STRENGTHS

- Calm, confident in face of adversity.
- Pioneers in new areas.
- Not afraid to take risks.
- Strong drive to achieve.
- Ambitious, competitive.

WEAKNESSES

- Overlooks advice of more cautious advisors.
- Can offend others with too much self-confidence.
- May take advantage of others' weaknesses.

vs

CAUTIOUS

STRENGTHS

- Takes cautious approach to life.
- Carefully weighs facts prior to making a decision.
- Sticks with "tried and true" plans that work.

WEAKNESSES

- Can be overprotective.
- Pessimistic, fearful.
- May procrastinate with decision-making.
- May lack initiative.

INNOVATIVE

STRENGTHS

- Quick-minded problem solver.
- Imaginative, original thinker.
- Outspoken in defending ideas.
- Clever, intellectual.

WEAKNESSES

- May harbor a critical or judgmental attitude.
- Bored easily with routine.
- Rebellious toward authority or established procedure.

vs

CONVENTIONAL

STRENGTHS

- Practical and realistic.
- Follows established rules.
- Very loyal and systematic.
- Excels at maintaining routines.
- Conservative, loyal to traditions.

WEAKNESSES

- May have a fear of failure.
- May underestimate abilities.
- Tends to be stressed by changes.

Keep in mind that a personality mismatch between the individual and the requirements of the job is one of the most common causes of career stress.

As a general rule, you are more successful when you operate from your strengths. On the other hand, remember that strengths overdone can become major flaws.

To be effective, you need a balance of behaviors. Yet it's not easy to modify the negative aspects of extremes. One of the constant themes of Scripture is that of balance and sensitivity to others. It is the Holy Spirit who changes us and empowers us to act more Christ-like. The apostle Paul is an excellent model. Among his many personality characteristics, a study of Scripture will reveal that he was extroverted, adventurous, dominant, detached, innovative, and conscientious. After his conversion, these same attributes still describe him, yet his increasing love and humility were clear indicators of a Spirit-filled life.

The key is to discover your God-given personality strengths and bring them under the Lordship of Jesus Christ. The best temperament is a Spirit-filled temperament.

It's important to know our general personality profile and to use our strengths, but we cannot excuse the negative aspects by saying "that's just the way I am."

Day by day, step by step, we are to surrender our rights in order to be in total submission to our Lord. Then He can use our talents to fulfill His purposes on earth.

WORK PRIORITIES AND VALUES

The center of the bull's eye, and probably the most important of the four areas we are discussing, is work priorities and values. Some areas of your priorities will overlap with your skills, vocational interests, and personality. The area that deals with your values, however, will be the acid test for your career decisions. Let me explain.

"But seek first His kingdom and His righteousness, and all these things will be given to you as well" (Matthew 6:33).

You could have two people with identical skills, interests, and personalities; yet one could be satisfied with a sales job while the other would hate it or even refuse to do it simply because of the values of the company or product. If the sales methods employed by the company were unfair or unethical, a Christian might reject the job while someone else became wealthy selling the product.

Taken to an extreme, you could imagine that leading a street gang and pioneering a new company would require a similar pattern—except for one key area: values. Such extremes are easy to see, but most people face decisions in the gray zone where it's not so clear and the temptations are great.

We can't emphasize enough: *Be strict with yourself in the area of values; rather than glossing over them, face up to them and make them a key criteria for your career decisions.*

You'll never regret honoring the values that have eternal and spiritual foundations.

You will find that your priorities will change as you go through life. Physical maturity, spiritual maturity, and changes in your circumstances will usually cause some reordering of your priorities. For that reason, you should periodically review your list and change your priorities as necessary.

DISCOVERING YOUR PATTERN FOR WORK

The Career Pathways method for career development takes into account your strengths in all four of these areas: work skills, vocational interests, personality, and work priorities and values. These four dimensions define your "pattern" for work.

Each dimension makes a valuable contribution to your understanding of God's plan for your life. For that reason, it is a mistake to formulate career plans and goals and overlook any of the four dimensions. For instance, I have a high level of interest in playing golf. I lack the skills, however, to excel in that game, and it would be a mistake to attempt to earn a living at that endeavor.

Or, you may have personality tendencies, skills, and interests that would enable you to excel in the field of sales. Your values, however, may prevent you from selling products that are potentially harmful. Increasingly, we're seeing Christians make career decisions based on key values in their lives, such as respect for biblical principles and allowing time for their families.

To make wise, responsible career decisions, you must consider how your skills, interests, personality, and values all complement one another. We have found it helpful to refer to a person's "pattern" for work using the pattern being defined by the four areas discussed earlier.

Carefully study the charts below, noting how people's patterns are comprised of their personalities, skills, vocational interests, and values. By matching their strengths to the job description, they can maximize use of their talents. Furthermore, notice that Person A's natural talents would be a mismatch for working as a carpenter, and Person B would not fit the counselor mold.

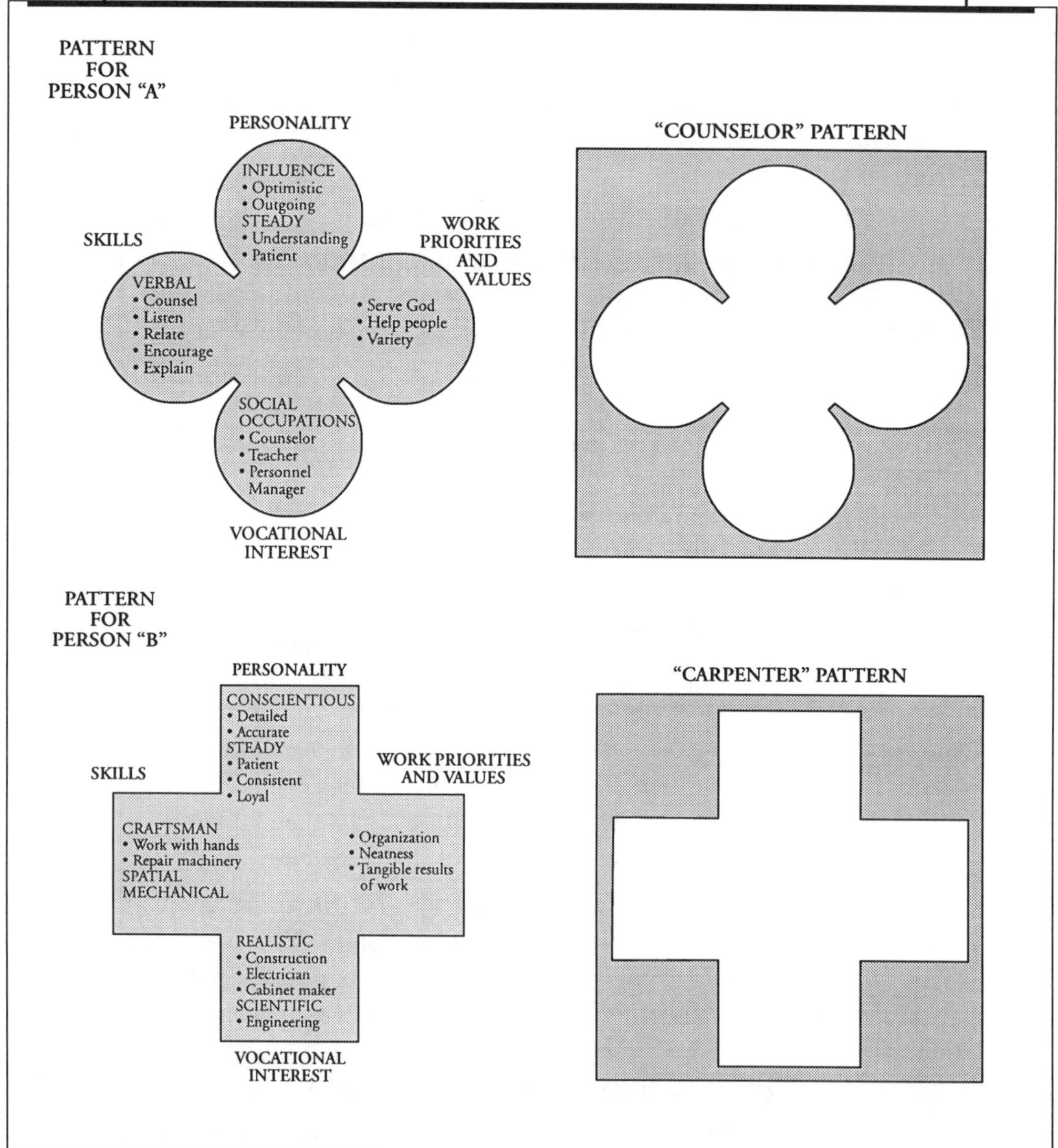

Developing Your Pattern

Before choosing a career you should have a good understanding of your pattern. A written description of "Your Pattern" is a key step for Career Pathways clients.

Following through on this important step will enable you to develop an accurate picture of how God has uniquely gifted you for work.

3 Defining Your Purpose

Your Purpose Statement

Life in the twentieth century has become so complex and so rushed that many of us are caught up in a merry-go-round of activity. Our focus is divided among many family concerns, social involvements, and professional responsibilities. We are further distracted by advertisements which saturate us with too many choices and lead us to unrealistic expectations about life and contentment. Without a plan it's difficult to make sound decisions, and it's easy for life to become chaotic and stressful.

"You are worthy, our Lord and God, to receive glory and honor and power, for you created all things, and by your will they were created and have their being" (Revelation 4:11).

The starting point for ordering your life and overcoming chaos is to develop a clear understanding of your life's purpose and the priorities and values that support that purpose. With a well-written purpose statement, you have a map that can guide you as you face choices at the crossroads of life.

In Chapter 2, you developed your pattern to determine "Who am I?" In this chapter, you'll write a purpose statement by looking at the "why" question: "Why am I here?" You'll also develop some priorities for key areas of your life, using your purpose statement as a foundation.

Your purpose statement is really an expression of why you exist and what you should be about on this earth. Also, since we can all anticipate an end to life on this earth, a good purpose statement should include what will be the outcome after death.

One caution to observe as you begin writing:

Be sure your purpose statement really reflects your desires and not what you think others would approve of.

"Many are the plans in a man's heart, but it is the Lord's purpose that prevails" (Proverbs 19:21).

You may not be able to live up to the full extension of your purpose, but it should reflect your beliefs, motivations, and desires. Out of your purpose will flow your values and priorities, which will determine the direction of your career and life pathways.

The following is **the primary purpose of my existence on this earth.**

____

____

____

____

____

In order to stay on track in fulfilling your purpose, consider how it will affect the following key areas.

My purpose will have the following effect on me **spiritually**.

____

____

____

"And we pray this in order that you may live a life worthy of the Lord and may please Him in every way; bearing fruit in every good work, growing in the knowledge of God" (Colossians 1:10).

In order to fulfill my purpose, I will need to set certain priorities to meet the needs of my **family**. Specifically, I will be guided by the following principles and priorities in my relationships.

With my spouse: ___________________________

____

____

____

____

____

With my children: _________________________

____

____

____

____

____

Since the major part of my waking hours are spent at **work**, I need to be sure my purpose is being accomplished in my work. In order to do that, I have established the following priorities for my **work**.

____

____

____

____

____

As a part of achieving my purpose, I believe that God has equipped me for the following areas of **ministry in my community**. Study Romans 12:6-8 and select your two or three strongest motivational gifts.

"There are different kinds of gifts, but the same Spirit" (1 Corinthians 12:4).

____ **a. Administrator/Leader:** Gives leadership and direction. Keeps things organized and increases others' visions.

____ **b. Perceiver/Knowledge (Prophecy):** Declares the will of God. Keeps others centered on spiritual principles.

____ **c. Server:** Renders practical service. Keeps the work of the ministry going.

____ **d. Compassion/Mercy:** Provides personal and emotional support. Reinforces right attitudes and relationships.

____ **e. Exhorter:** Encourages personal progress. Exhorts others to apply spiritual truths.

____ **f. Teacher:** Researches and teaches the Bible. Keeps the focus on studying and learning.

____ **g. Giver:** Shares material assistance. Provides for specific needs.

I will use my **primary gift** to fulfill my purpose by:

____

____

____

____

____

I will use my **secondary gift** to fulfill my purpose by:

"Be sure you know the condition of your flocks, give careful attention to your herds" (Proverbs 27:23).

Finances will have an key impact on the way I go about achieving my purpose in life. My guiding philosophy regarding money and finances could be described best in the following statements.

My **character and integrity** will be a major determinant in successfully achieving my purpose. The following statements describe the kind of person I want to be.

"I want to know Christ and the power of His resurrection and the fellowship of sharing in His sufferings, becoming like Him in His death, and so, somehow, to attain to the resurrection from the dead" (Philippians 3:10-11).

My life's purpose will affect my plans for **eternity** (life after death) in the following ways.

I recognize the need for **godly counsel** in my life as I plan and try to balance the many areas of my life. Listed below are the names of trusted confidants I will seek out to be my counselors. I will apprise them of my situation and seek their wisdom. Most important, I will ask them to pray with and for me.

My **prayer partners**: ______________________

____

____

____

____

____

"Therefore confess your sins to each other and pray for each other so that you may be healed. The prayer of a righteous man is powerful and effective" (James 5:16).

Others who will pray for me: ______________________

____

____

____

____

____

Since your purpose statement will be a guide in your actions and decisions, you'll want to review it from time to time. It may also change as you grow in wisdom and truth.

This chapter originally completed ______________________.
(date)

This chapter reviewed ______________________. ◆
(date)

"Choosing a career is not a one-time decision; it's a series of decisions, made as you progress through the seasons and experiences of life. As the expression goes, we would rather teach you to how to fish (make your own decisions) than give you a fish, (decide for you). In fact, if you can learn to fish (make good career decisions) and then teach someone else, maybe a lot of the employment, productivity, and even spiritual problems that Christians struggle with today could be resolved."[1]

Lee Ellis

[1]Larry Burkett and Lee Ellis, *Your Career in Changing Times*. Chicago: Moody Press, 1993, p 142.

4 Making Career Decisions

In *Finding Your Mission in Life* (Ten Speed Press), Richard Bolles discusses the need to unlearn the errors we have learned and then learn the truths. That is the purpose of this chapter. First we will look at what we need to unlearn about choosing a career; then we will outline some steps that have proved to be successful.

How to Make Bad Career Decisions

1. Choose the first/easiest job you can get. This is the slothful way out and it is certainly not being a good steward of your talents. When you ignore your God-given talents, aren't you putting yourselves in a similar situation as the servant who buried his talents (in the parable Jesus related in Matthew 25:14-30)?

"The sluggard craves and gets nothing, but the desires of the diligent are fully satisfied" (Proverbs 13:4).

It is likely there will be times in all of our careers when we may take interim jobs just to put food on the table, but our goals should always be to move into areas where we are using our strongest talents in our work.

2. Choose a job based on the amount of money it pays. We have already discussed this in Chapter 1; however, this error is so established in our culture it's going to require a real measure of faith for most people to actually choose a job on any other basis. It is the attraction of materialism and our pride that causes us to want more and more. If you haven't gone through Larry Burkett's workbook, *How to Manage Your Money* (Moody), we strongly encourage you to do so. This Bible study on money provides the biblical foundation that will increase your faith and allow you to learn to be content at whatever economic level God calls you.

"Whoever loves money never has money enough; whoever loves wealth is never satisfied with his income. This too is meaningless" (Ecclesiastes 5:10).

3. Choose a job because it sounds like a good title. Have you noticed how companies have changed the names of jobs to make them sound more important? One discount store calls its cashiers "terminal operators," and I'm sure you have noticed the emphasis our society places on having a good "position." Doing what you're good at and what you enjoy is usually a far better way to choose a job than just selecting a title.

"Better to be a nobody and yet have a servant than pretend to be somebody and have no food" (Proverbs 12:9).

A friend of mine told me recently, "I am fortunate because I love my work. I have variety, I am outdoors, I get to help people, and I'm my own boss." Many people would not want his job, however, because he pumps out septic tanks. I admire this man for what he does and for the way he honors the Lord in his work. There are many people who have impressive titles, but they hate their work and would give anything to love their work like my friend does.

"A simple man believes anything, but a prudent man gives thought to his steps" (Proverbs 14:15).

4. Take a job just because management offers it. We see this happen repeatedly in the lives of our Career Pathways clients. For example, consider men and women who excel in their production work. They love to work with their hands. And they do such a good job of it, upper management decides to promote them to management level jobs.

So instead of doing what they love the most, they accept the new promotion and oversee others doing the work. In the new position, the employee must solve people problems, train others to do the work, be responsible for the work of others, meet quotas, and report to higher officials. Far too often the promotion only leads to stress and frustration.

Don't take a job just because upper management offers it. Many managers still don't comprehend the wisdom of matching people to their work. Upper management might simply be trying to fill a management slot, and that job description may or may not match your talents. Carefully evaluate promotions in light of your God-given strengths and your pattern for work. If it's a match, go for it. If it's not a match, however, why be promoted to a job that's an obvious mismatch for you and one that's certain to draw from your weaknesses?

5. Choose a job because that's what your parents do. One Career Pathways client's dad was a chemical engineer and his mom was a biologist. He grew up believing that "real jobs" were to be found in the sciences or law. His parents never told him that outright; he just assumed it. So the young man struggled to prepare for a career in law. He hated the studies, fought constant discouragement, toiled endlessly for average grades, and finally quit law school.

In desperation, he took the Career Pathways career assessments, which pointed him toward careers in the arts. This young man recently graduated with a 4.0, with a degree in professional and technical writing. A letter from his college professor attests to his superior qualifications; he was one of the best to ever graduate from that university in that department.

Don't choose a career track just because that's what your parents do. You may be 40 and just discovering what a tremendous shadow of influence your parents have had on your career planning.

God has created you to be unique. Discover that uniqueness and develop your career plans around it.

6. Choose a job to fulfill your parents' unfulfilled dreams. Parents must be very careful not to steer their children to something the parents would like. Career encouragement without thorough consideration of the child's God-given pattern usually causes serious stress in the child. Even though they don't always show it, young people generally want to please their parents. So if your parents have pushed you in one direction and your natural bent is in another, the problems can be serious.

"There are different kinds of working, but the same God works all of them in all men" (1 Corinthians 12:6).

Many college students delay choosing a major and even suffer clinical depression because they are unable to resolve a conflict between their parents' desires and their natural bent. Parents need to remember they are not owners; rather, they are stewards, rearing a future adult.

7. Choose a job just because you have the minimum ability to do it. God created humans as very special and highly developed organisms, so we all have many basic abilities. There are many jobs we "can" do, but they are not necessarily God's plan for us. Usually His plan also involves our strongest skills, our personalities and, even more important, our motivations. He causes some areas to appeal to us more than others, and these usually are related to the career field in which He would have us shine for Him.

"Delight yourself in the Lord and he will give you the desires of your heart" (Psalm 37:4).

How to Make Good Career Decisions

1. First clarify your purpose in life. For the Christian, the fundamental question is: Do I really trust my life to God's hands? Am I willing to relinquish control to Him? Since God wants what is best for us, and He has shown us over and over that He cares, then why not let Him be in command? Why not commit to being a servant in His kingdom for His honor and glory?

We are not capable of perfectly living up to that commitment but, praise the Lord, we don't have to. He merely asks us to commit (to make it our will) to trust and obey, and then He sends the Holy Spirit to help us (see John 16:5-15).

Once you've clarified your purpose, *outline some goals based on what you stand for and what you want the end results of your work to be.* You've been given talents and a life to live; this is the "so what am I going to do with it" question that will serve as your compass in life. You already should have answered this in Chapter 3. If you haven't done so, go back now and work through that chapter.

"For we are God's workmanship, created in Christ Jesus to do good works, which God prepared in advance for us to do" (Ephesians 2:10).

2. Learn about your natural "bent." This includes as a minimum your abilities, interests, personality strengths, and your priorities and values. Learning about your bent is the primary purpose of the Career Pathways assessment program. A written description of "Your Pattern" will give you a good picture of your God-given strengths.

"For lack of guidance a nation falls, but many advisers make victory sure" (Proverbs 11:14).

3. Investigate/explore several occupations that fit "Your Pattern." Using your pattern, you can concentrate your search on the jobs that potentially are a good fit. Read, interview people, and visit work sites in order to identify jobs that best match your pattern. You have nothing to lose and everything to gain through your efforts. Don't miss out on your niche because you didn't take the time to find it.

4. Seek God's confirmation. By now you should begin to see possibilities in these occupations. Continue to pray specifically for God's direction in your search and His leading in your decision. Share your information with other Christians who know you well, and seek their counsel. Trust that God will help you make your choice. Wait until He gives you peace about your decision.

"The plans of the diligent lead to profit as surely as haste leads to poverty" (Proverbs 21:5).

5. Choose your direction and your initial destination and develop a plan to get there. If necessary, prepare yourself through education and training to reach your goal. When you develop your talents you are like the servants who invested their talents and doubled them during the master's absence (see Matthew 25:14-30).

6. Become a lifelong learner, always gathering new ideas about your work and its related fields. We are to study both the Bible and our vocations in order to show ourselves approved. Our society has moved through the agricultural age, the industrial age, and now is in the information age. Farmers and industrial workers are now using computers and advanced technology in order to compete. Reading, taking courses, and further training are a way of life for those who want to shine at work.

7. Refine your career as you go along. After you're in a job you'll see areas in which you can grow and develop. Prepare, and move along when the doors open. Be careful not to move up into an area that does not suit your strengths. We often see employees move into management because it looks like a good "career move," only to discover the stress of being mismatched to their new jobs.

The Role of Prayer in Decision Making

We cannot leave the subject of decision making without emphasizing the importance of prayer. Prayer is a powerful way that God has ordained for us to operate in the supernatural spiritual realm on this earth. When we neglect prayer, not only are we being disobedient, we are shortchanging God and ourselves of His best for us. In prayer He molds our hearts to His perfect will, and it is through prayer that He changes the hearts of others and even the very circumstances around us. We must pray, pray, and continue to pray so that our hearts are tuned in to His message for us.

"Many are the plans in a man's heart, but it is the Lord's purpose that prevails" (Proverbs 19:21).

HOW TO PRAY

1. Create a prayer agenda for each scheduled prayer time. This can range from a brief list of names and job leads to more extensive journal notes. As you compile this agenda, don't allow your career issues to consume your entire prayer life. Maintain balance in your devotions by concentrating on God's character, as well as on the needs of others. As difficult as it may sound, life goes on in spite of your career transition, and God desires to touch the lives of others through you.

2. File your past prayer agendas. By keeping track of them, you will be able to see answers to your prayers as time passes. This can become a real source of encouragement to you and your spouse.

3. Ask God for an open heart to His Word. According to Psalm 1, the person who delights in the law of the Lord *"is like a tree planted by streams of water, which yields its fruit in season and whose leaf does not wither. Whatever he does prospers"* (Psalm 1:3). Like seeds sown in a garden, the principles from God's word will sprout up, bearing the fruits of righteousness, peace, and purpose in your life.

4. Praise God for His faithfulness to you and your family. If you cannot discern His provision for you, ask Him to show you how He's providing. One of His names is *Jehovah-Jireh,* meaning "Jehovah's provision shall be seen."

WE ALL NEED PRAYER PARTNERS

We are to pray alone, but we also need to have prayer partners. We need the support of our spouses, our families, our friends, and we also need a same-sex prayer partner. There is something very special and very encouraging about a prayer partner. If you don't have one, get one, and meet at least once a week to share and pray together.

"Trust in the Lord with all your heart and lean not on your own understanding; in all your ways acknowledge Him, and He will make your paths straight" (Proverbs 3:5-6).

A Framework for Decision Making

In counseling at Christian Financial Concepts and Career Pathways, we've observed over and over a systematic plan for discovering God's will. This method works for career, financial, or any other type decision-making situation. As you can see, usually this is not an overnight process; rather, it's a walk in faith.

Trust - Faith

Our Role—Process	***God's Role—Results***
• **Submit and commit to follow God's call**	• **Open doors**
• **Pray for His will and wisdom**	• **Close doors**
• **Work the process –** Assessment, résumé, investigation, job search, and so on	• **Confirm His will**
• **Seek godly counsel**	
• **Exercise patience — wait**	• **Give us peace**
• **Make choices based on the steps above**	• **Produce results**
• **Glorify God**	• **Glorify His name**

Holy Spirit

Note: Items on each side not intended to be parallel.

Too often we work things backward. We decide on the results *we* want and then pray that God will bless us and make them happen. When we do this we deny Him full control, and we deny ourselves His full blessings. Turning the results over to Him is a critical, but necessary, step if we are going to know His will. ◆

5 Gaining Wisdom for a Career Transition

Considering a career transition is often a crisis situation. The transition can be more of a "controlled" crisis when you have a year's advance warning of layoffs, or it can be more of an "abrupt" crisis, if you receive a pink slip at 4:55 p.m. on Friday. Either way, a career transition begets change, and increased levels of stress usually accompany major life changes.

The key in all of this is to make wise decisions. All of us like to make decisions today that we'll still be pleased with 10 years from now. And, even though no one is perfect, careful and prayerful preparation can minimize mistakes and help us to avoid hasty, impulsive choices. Wise decisions are highly valued commodities and are possible to achieve.

Five Steps to Making A Wise Career Transition

1. Earnestly seek wisdom. Prayerfully and earnestly make this a priority in your life. Seek to understand your circumstances from God's point of view. God has promised in His word that He will grant wisdom to those who ask (James 1:5-8) . . . so ask! The career decision you're facing is only one small component of God's overall plan for your life. The early chapters of Proverbs will be a true inspiration for you in your search for wisdom.

"If any of you lacks wisdom, he should ask God, who gives generously to all without finding fault, and it will be given to him. But when he asks, he must believe and not doubt, because he who doubts is like a wave of the sea, blown and tossed by the wind. That man should not think he will receive anything from the Lord, he is a double-minded man, unstable in all he does" (James 1:5-8).

2. Exercise faith. Even when you have done all the research possible on the career transition, there comes a moment of decision when you must step out in faith. You cannot predict your future. You never can amass all the information necessary. In spite of your very best efforts, it is possible that you will fail.

The good news is, God not only blesses our best efforts, but He also redeems our failures. Redemption, the capacity to make something good out of something bad, is God's business. Look what He did with the cross: He turned it into the resurrection. And consider how He brought you to salvation. So at the very worst, God is able to handle even our biggest mistakes and worst failures.

Hebrews 11:6 tells us, *"And without faith, it is impossible to please God."* That being true, why should you be surprised when He calls you to step out in faith? He knows you don't have all the answers. He knows you cannot peer into tomorrow. You don't have to. He's already there. Jesus is the eternal One. Do all you can; then trust Him for the outcome.

Very likely you are familiar with the story of the apostle Peter walking on the water in response to the beckoning of the Lord Jesus. The story is found in Matthew 14:33. At the call of Jesus, Peter stepped away from the safety and security of the boat and began walking across the water to Jesus. He was fine until he took his eyes off the Lord, and then he began to sink. "Save me!" Peter cried to Jesus. And, of course, Jesus rescued him from harm's way.

It's better to be knee deep in water while holding on to the hand of Jesus than it is to be in the boat without Him. Likewise, it's better to step out in faith with Jesus in your career decision than it is to resist His Spirit and remain in the safety of what you have now. This, of course, presumes you sense the Lord beckoning you forth into a career transition.

3. Commit yourself to action. You can think about career changes for the rest of your life. Thinking is important but, in and of itself, it won't get the job done. There comes a time to decide. There comes a time to act.

For Moses, the time came under stressful conditions. Pharoah's army was closing in from the West. Nothing but water on the East. Deep water. The only alternative was to do what God said to do. He stretched out his staff over the waters of the Red Sea . . . and God split them wide open. Notice that ***nothing*** happened until Moses acted upon what God told him to do.

It's not uncommon for people to become immobilized by what we call "paralysis by analysis." They become so caught up in analyzing the circumstances that they cannot come to a point of decision. They get lost in a forest of facts.

Hold yourself accountable to someone for making a commitment, even if that commitment is to remain in your present work.

4. Seek out a mentor. One of the real blessings of working on the Career Pathways staff comes from mentoring relationships in the office. We teach one another. We challenge one another. For the sake of Christ, we submit to one another. And the result is we usually raise our performance a notch or two. We've discovered that we can do better if we candidly ***entrust ourselves to one another and to the Lord.*** The biblical principle behind our mentoring relationships says, *"Iron sharpens iron, so one man sharpens another"* (Proverbs 27:17).

As you process all the relevant factors to your career transition, we highly encourage you to seek out a mentor to whom you will be accountable. You might have several mentors: one to oversee your financial transition, one to assist you with this particular career transition chapter, and another to help you evaluate your strengths and weaknesses for work.

Don't overlook the importance of obtaining a wise, godly mentor during a career transition. One of the contributing factors to mental depression is isolation. It's no secret that job loss is frequently associated with shame or guilt in our society. Those are powerful emotional forces that cause us to withdraw from our support base of friends and family. This kind of isolation quickly commences a spiraling effect that leads to deeper and deeper depression. Don't fall into this trap. Being accountable to a mentor can help you remain strong, persistent, and actively involved in your job search.

5. Persist in the battle. Seldom are wars won by one battle. Instead, they are won by systematic campaigns which are composed of persistent efforts. Sometimes there are setbacks. Things may look gloomy from time to time, and "the enemy" may appear to have the upper hand.

In those times, remember that God has called you to be responsible to work the process, and He will produce the results. Give it your best in your current work. Discover and refine your talents to shine the brightest. Network like you know everyone in the business. Whittle that résumé down to a sharp, impressive finish. Research that new company, and practice for that upcoming interview. And when you've done everything you can do, trust God to work out the results.

Failure is not the result of a layoff or rejected résumé. Neither is it being passed over on the short list of interviews. Failure comes from giving up, not even trying, quenching the spirit of hope within you that prompts you to excel. Failure closes God out of the picture by telling Him that He's not even big enough to handle the situation.

Persist! As the great British statesman, Winston Churchill once said, "Never quit. Never, never, never, never, never, never, never, never quit."

You do your part and trust God to do His.

▶▶ Five Elements of a Wise Decision

A wise decision is:

1. Made with all the relevant facts at hand that are possible to obtain. A wise decision has been soundly researched. *"It is not good to have zeal without knowledge, nor to be hasty and miss the way"* (Proverbs 19:2).

2. Consistent with the principles from God's word. Study the Bible with an eye to specific counsel concerning life purpose and work issues. *"Your word is a lamp to my feet and a light for my path"* (Psalm 119:105).

3. Made after thoughtful interaction with your spouse (if you're married). *"Submit to one another out of reverence for Christ"* (Ephesians 5:21).

4. Informed by godly counsel. Seek the reflections of your pastor and respected Christian friends. *"For waging war you need guidance, and for victory many advisers"* (Proverbs 24:6).

5. Molded by the power of the Holy Spirit. Jesus said, *"But when he, the Spirit of truth, comes, he will guide you into all truth"* (John 16:13).

Considering the Larger Picture

"Suppose one of you wants to build a tower. Will he not first sit down and estimate the cost to see if he has enough money to complete it? For if he lays the foundation and is not able to finish it, everyone who sees it will ridicule him, saying, 'This fellow began to build and was not able to finish.' " (Luke 14:28-30).

By incorporating these principles into your career planning, you have taken some important steps toward making wise decisions about your career development. You should have a clear picture of your personality strengths, skills, vocational interests, and values. These four areas are critical to the formation of your unique pattern for work (see chapter 2). Information in these areas is like an inner X ray of you, revealing the strengths God has endowed to you and the values that drive your desire to work.

The remaining issue is, how can you make wise career decisions based on this information? If you suddenly find yourself stumped, you're not alone. There are additional factors to consider when planning a career transition beyond your pattern. Seldom are people free to strike out on a new career direction based only on new insights about themselves. There are other factors to contend with, many of which complicate our career plans or entangle us. The diagram below illustrates some of these factors.

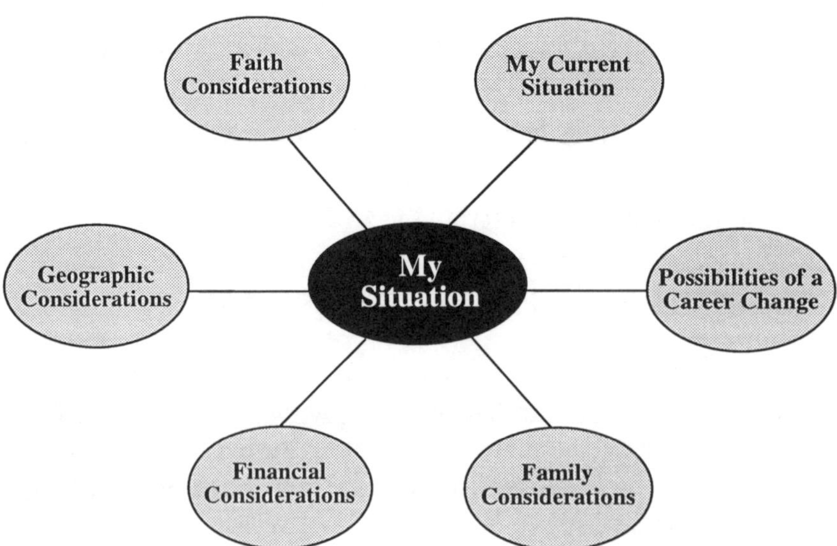

For instance, you may have to consider a host of personal financial factors. If your spouse is working, you should take into account how your job change will affect him or her. If a new job requires you to move from one region of the country to another, you must evaluate those factors, especially if you're moving away from extended family.

Indeed, a survey of more than 4,500 transfering employees and their families, published by the *National Business Employment Weekly*, shows that the largest hurdles to overcome in a career transition are personal issues and not job-related issues. Almost three-fifths (58 percent) of the respondents said their most pressing problems following a relocation concerned psychological or emotional factors.[1] Examples include missing your church family, favorite restaurant, support base of friends, the kids adjusting to new schools, and so on. You can see that there are a wide range of issues to consider and evaluate when making a job change.

To help you further assess these additional factors, we have developed a series of questions for you to consider as part of your career planning. By answering these questions, you are working through the same process we would follow if we were providing personal counseling.

Since most people don't have a career counselor, we re-emphasize the importance of a mentor, a respected, mature Christian from your sphere of fellowship, who can oversee you as you complete these questions. We cannot overstate the importance of a mentor. You may very well be approaching the most critical, dynamic steps of your career transition. This is the analytical stage, in which you synthesize all the study information you've been exposed to. If Satan were to throw up any road blocks in the process, here's where he'll attack with discouragement and distraction. He may attempt to convince you that you've done enough by discovering how God has made you. But the truth is, God wants you to both ***discover and apply*** what you've learned for His sake and His work here on earth.

Frankly, there are usually only a few key transition points in our lives when so much is at stake. You may be standing at such a crossroads yourself right now. You literally will be living out the consequences of the current career decision for years to come. Having a mentor at this stage of your career transition is a wise step to take. Just do it.

Carefully work through the following pages to consider the many factors relevant to your career decisions.

1. ASSESS YOUR CURRENT SITUATION

Use the space below to identify the factors you are most pleased with in your current work. Will new opportunities offer similar qualities and opportunities?

Use the space below to identify the factors causing you the most stress in your current work. As you investigate new opportunities, be sure to evaluate whether the factors will be present.

Are other, non-career factors prompting the possible job change? If so, what are they?

What God-given talents are you using in your current work?

What God-given talents are being underused in your current work?

How does your current work stress affect your family life?

How does your current work stress affect your spiritual life?

____

____

____

____

NOTE: If you have taken the Career Pathways Career Assessment, the insights from your personality report will help you to clarify your strengths and weaknesses below.

Use the following lines to identify your natural strengths that will help you in making a career transition.

____

____

____

____

____

____

Use the following lines to identify your natural weaknesses that may complicate your ability to make a career transition.

____

____

____

____

____

____

On a scale of 1 to 10, where 1 is neglected and 10 is superior, evaluate your personal lifestyle habits in the following areas:

____ Leisure ____ Family time

____ Diet habits ____ Ministry time in your church

____ Exercise

How do you anticipate these areas will be affected by a new job opportunty?

____

____

2. ASSESS THE POSSIBILITIES OF A CAREER CHANGE

What risks do you face by remaining in your current job?

What counsel are you receiving from your peers in your field about making a job change? List specific encouragements and reservations. Record insights from three people.

1.

2.

3.

Have you clearly articulated your career goals? In the space below, state at least one short-term goal (within months), one intermediate goal (6 months to 5 years), and one long-range goal (5 years to 20 years).

What are the risks involved in making a job change at this time in your life?

Have you reviewed a job description for the position you are considering? If so, how does it match your God-given talents, skills, interests, and values? How does it compare to your present position? How will it be different?

3. FAMILY CONSIDERATIONS

(Respond as applicable)

Does your spouse support you changing jobs? List his or her key pro and con points. Use space below to summarize.

____

____

____

____

____

____

Will your job change necessitate a change of jobs for your spouse? In the space below, summarize your spouse's outlook and attitude about changing his or her job.

____

____

____

____

____

____

Are there specific, unresolved issues between you and your spouse regarding a job change? What are they, and what is your plan to address these issues?

____

____

____

____

Will your job change result in a move or your children changing schools? In the space below, summarize each child's concerns (if appropriate). Example: Susie will have to quit the cheerleading team; John may jeopardize a college scholarship if he quits the basketball team.

____

____

____

____

____

____

Will your modes of transportation change because of a new job?

____

Will your job change result in a change in work schedule? If so, will this require new child-care arrangements?

____

What benefits will the new job offer? vacation? sick time? family emergency time?

____

____

____

____

Will changing jobs alter your health care benefits package? If so, how? What financial impact will this have for your family?

____

____

____

____

4. EDUCATIONAL CONSIDERATIONS

Will the new job require more education or new certification on your part? If so, what are the new qualifications and how will you meet them?

____

____

____

How will you pay for more course work?

____

Approximately how long will it take for you to obtain this education, training, or certification? On a scale of 1 to 10, where 1 is impossible and 10 is highly probable, evaluate and rank your likelihood of completing the training at this stage in your life.

____

____

Are you qualified for admission into a new degree program? (Note: You may have to meet with college representatives or review a college catalog to answer this question.)

____

Will you be taking evening classes? If so, where?

____

How will evening classes impact your family time with spouse and children?

____

____

____

Will you have to arrange for child care while you're in class?

____

5. FINANCIAL CONSIDERATIONS

How will the new job pay? twice a month? once a month?

____

What will your take-home pay be?

____

Will you have to work one complete pay period before drawing a check?

____

How will you pay expenses prior to your first check?

____

How will your new pay rate impact your ability to pay off past loans, credit cards, or other debts? List adjustments you will have to make below.

____

____

____

____

How will a job change impact your retirement plans? Will you be losing seniority?

____

How will your old and new budgets compare if you take a new job?

____

Are you fully invested in your company's retirement plans? What steps will you take to roll over your current retirement plans to a new plan?

Will your new company be paying all or a portion of your moving expenses? If not, list your anticipated moving expenses below, along with an estimate of each cost.

If you are paying a portion of your moving expenses, do you have sufficient savings reserves to cover these costs?

If you are moving, have you calculated the cost-of-living expenses in areas of food, housing, utilities, and insurance? Other factors?

6. GEOGRAPHIC CONSIDERATIONS

Will the new job require you to move?

Will the new job necessitate selling your home?

What impact will moving have on your children?

What impact will moving have on your relationships with parents, in-laws, and extended family?

Are there areas of the country where you don't want to live (allergies, harsh winters, hurricanes, and so forth)?

Will you move while the children are in school or wait until summer break?

Will your new community have recreation facilities/activities available?

What have you learned about the political and moral climate of your new community?

If you move, will your children be homeschooled? attend Christian school? private school? public school? If public school, how does the new school district rank with the rest of the state?

7. FAITH CONSIDERATIONS

What counsel do your pastor and church leaders offer?

Identify and list the Scripture passages that are most meaningful and insightful to you in this decision-making process.

Describe what will it mean for you to leave your current church home?

What church leadership responsibilities will you be vacating if you move?

What kind of church will you be looking for in a new community? What factors do you regard as "essential" as you look for a new church family?

____
____
____
____
____
____

If you are electing to change jobs, how are you different from Jonah, who sought to avoid circumstances by changing locations?

____
____
____
____

Do you have personal fears or concerns to address when making a job change? What about your spouse? List them below.

____
____
____
____
____
____

List people below who are serving as a prayer-support team to intercede for you while considering this change.

____
____
____

Are you consistent in your "quiet times" with the Lord in Bible study and prayer? Summarize what the Lord is teaching you through your circumstances in the space below.

____
____
____
____
____
____

Are there any attitudes or behaviors present in your life that are contrary to God's written word? Any that could complicate your ability to understand how God is leading you?

____

____

You have now evaluated seven factors relevant to making a career transition. As pictured in the diagram below, you can see how each of these factors will influence your ability to make a career transition.

To summarize what you have discovered, use the space below to identify any remaining barriers to your career progress. Be as specific as you can, and use extra paper if necessary. Some sections may have a number of remaining obstacles, and you may have no entries in some sections.

You are also provided space to identify decisions that must be made about the obstacles, along with target dates for making the decision. Since these details may change from time to time, consider this section a "working document" to be completed in pencil.

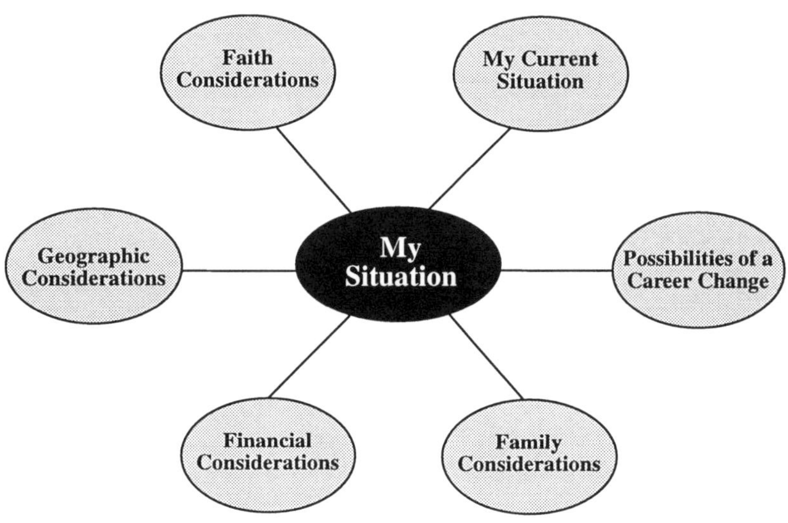

1. MY CURRENT SITUATION

a. Obstacles to overcome:

____

____

____

b. Decisions to make, along with target dates:

___

___

___

"And without faith it is impossible to please God, because anyone who comes to him must believe that he exists and that he rewards those who earnestly seek him" (Hebrews 11:6).

2. POSSIBILITIES OF A CAREER CHANGE

a. Obstacles to overcome:

___

___

___

b. Decisions to make, along with target dates:

___

___

___

3. FAMILY CONSIDERATIONS

a. Obstacles to overcome:

___

___

___

b. Decisions to make, along with target dates:

___

___

___

4. EDUCATIONAL CONSIDERATIONS

a. Obstacles to overcome:

___

___

___

b. Decisions to make, along with target dates:

___

___

___

5. FINANCIAL CONSIDERATIONS

a. Obstacles to overcome:

____

____

____

b. Decisions to make, along with target dates:

____

____

____

6. GEOGRAPHIC CONSIDERATIONS

a. Obstacles to overcome:

____

____

____

b. Decisions to make, along with target dates:

____

____

____

7. FAITH CONSIDERATIONS

a. Obstacles to overcome:

____

____

____

b. Decisions to make, along with target dates:

____

____

____

In addition to the previous seven factors, you may have other significant matters to consider when making a career decision. Use the spaces below to identify additional obstacles to overcome and decisions to make.

8. FACTOR ______________________

a. Obstacles to overcome:

____

____

____

b. Decisions to make, along with target dates:

____

____

____

9. FACTOR ______________________

a. Obstacles to overcome:

____

____

____

b. Decisions to make, along with target dates:

____

____

____

ENDNOTES

1. Paul Hobson-Panico and Michael F. Tucker, "What You Can Expect During a Relocation," reprinted from *The National Employment Weekly,* published by *The Wall Street Journal,* p.3.

6 Keys to Employment in the 21st Century

Introduction to Change

The saying goes that there are three kinds of people in the world: those that **make** things happen, those that **watch** it happen, and those who **never knew** it happened.

The cutting edge for workers moving into the 21st century belongs to workers who make things happen. Two key characteristics (which in some ways are opposites) describe the worker who will thrive in this rapidly changing work world: focus and versatility.

One key element for 21st century workers will be the ability to focus their work on the natural strengths and talents God has uniquely provided them. This will require a thorough knowledge of these talents. Unsure workers will flounder, as focused workers keep pace with the changing work scene.

Versatility is the second key to competence. It's not enough to simply know how God has created us. In addition, we must be able to quickly discern how to use our God-given talents in new work settings.

When playing football, we called this simple strategy "read and react" on defense. When the football was snapped to the quarterback, the defense immediately had to "read" where the play was headed. Properly read, the next step involved reacting to the play development in time to make the tackle.

Ten Major Trends

Armed with a knowledge of our God-given strengths, workers moving into the 21st century must "read and react" to changes in order to compete. This necessarily means taking initiative and responsibility for personal career development, rather than waiting for the work world to seek you out.

For this reason, we have compiled a number of major trends that are reshaping the work world around us. As you review them, do your best to discover implications for you and your career development.

1. BECOMING A GLOBAL VILLAGE

We've seen the 1990s bring about rapid changes in worldwide trade policies, with the ratification of major treaties like NAFTA resulting in a complex, interdependent global market. The United States signed into the NAFTA and GATT treaties.

No longer operating within independent, nationalistic cultures, the work forces of industrialized and Third World nations have begun to collide. The 350 million workers in industrialized nations, whose pay averages $18 an hour, are suddenly competing with the 1.2 billion workers in Third World nations whose wages average less than $2 an hour.[1] The result has been abrupt changes in trade policy.

Workers who are adept at using high tech communications will be in demand. Likewise, those who become proficient in a second or third language will hold the edge in the competitive, global work force. Increasingly, corporations will need to grow in knowledge and sensitivity to once remote cultures.

2. FURTHER CORPORATE DOWNSIZING

As global networking increases, market prices will remain steady in order to remain competitive. Expect cost-cutting measures and layoffs to continue in an effort to maintain corporate profits. In addition, the growing and efficient use of technology will permanently replace many workers. Losses in the manufacturing sector, along with textiles, farming, and mid-management jobs, will be substantial.

Particularly vulnerable are middle-management men. Typically they are paid 20 percent more than women in the same positions.[2] And, while seniority used to be an asset, it now may very well be a liability. Business workers with the same company for more than 10 years are paid roughly 30 percent more than those hired more recently.[3] It's no surprise then to see this group on the chopping block first in the quest for corporate savings.

3. MORE WORK FOR FEWER WORKERS

Fewer laid-off workers will be replaced. Instead, remaining staff will be required to take up the slack, resulting in a heavier work load. So far, the strategy is working. For example, companies are now able to produce a ton of steel with only 2.3 worker hours, compared to 10.8 in 1982. Today, Caterpillar generates $2.3 million in sales per employee, compared to $886,000 in 1982.[4]

4. TALENT BECOMES FOCUS FOR JOB SECURITY

Job security is a relic of the past. In the old workplace model, security came with the company. Not any more. Job security in the future belongs to the worker who develops a track record of being "excellent" at a skill that is in demand. An employee's productivity and quality makes him or her a necessity to the economic success of a business or organization. Each work day has a direct effect on profitability. Workers are expected to contribute daily.

According to *The Washington Times,* 50 percent of the jobs that will exist in the year 2004 haven't even been created yet.[5] In such rapidly changing work conditions, security rests in the clear knowledge of your God-given talents and compatible work settings in which to use them.

Being mismatched in your work lowers productivity, morale, and often, quality of work. Not exactly the description for job security.

5. RAPID INCREASES IN TECHNOLOGY

Ten years ago, 25 percent of American workers used a computer on the job according to the Bureau of Labor Statistics. Today, that number is nearly 50 percent.[6]

In the seven years from 1987 to 1994, more than 10 million fax machines were purchased. E-mail addresses increased by more than 26 million.[7]

Time is money. Access to information is money. Increasingly sophisticated technology delivers information faster. Anticipate faster, more frequent changes due to more efficient use of technology. And if you haven't already, take a class in computers.

6. HOME BASED BUSINESSES GROW IN POPULARITY

Nearly 20 percent of workers who are laid off choose to start their own business.[8] New businesses were started in the United States in 1994 at an annual rate of 737,000.[9] Home based business is now the fastest growing sector of the economy, and the number is expected to double through the decade of the 90s.

Starting your own home business may require substantial financial and time resources. Be sure your family is braced for the adjustment. A survey of first-year business owners revealed that 50 percent worked between 50 and 70 hours a week; 25 percent worked more than 70 hours; only 13 percent worked between 40 and 49 hours.[10]

Chapter 10 of the PathFinder has some helpful tips if you are considering this step.

7. TELECOMMUTING FROM HOME

As workers continue to become empowered to make decisions and work independently on projects, the feasibility of working from home offices increases. Technological advances have made home office work as simple as a PC and modem.

Roughly one-third of America's work force, some 43 million people, are working at least part-time from home, up from 21 percent in 1988.[11]

The trend will continue for a time, but watch for it to level off. Humans are incredibly social creatures and many will crave the dynamics of the office. Some home workers have expressed shock over suddenly discovering the absence of support services available at the home office, but not at their home: administrative support, brainstorming sessions, copy and fax machines.

8. PREPARATION FOR WORK IS ESSENTIAL

U.S. Department of Labor statistics tell the story of how important a college education is for future earnings:

MEDIAN U.S. SALARIES	
High school graduate	$21,241
Bachelors degree	$34,385
Masters degree	$40,666
PhD degree	$52,403
Professional degree	$67,131[12]

Generally speaking, the demand for 21st century workers will more likely be for generalists who have specialist capabilities; and, a college degree will provide broad equipping for work.

A word of caution is appropriate here. A college degree is no guarantee of a good job. In fact, one in six current college graduates takes a job that doesn't require a college degree. And that ratio is expected to climb to one in every four college graduates in the next decade.

There appears to be two exceptions to the necessity of the college degree. One is to start your own business as an entrepreneur. A recent survey of highly successful U.S. entrepreneuers indicates that only 46 percent received their college degrees; 29 percent never went to college; and 27 percent started college but never finished.[13]

The second exception to the college degree is learning a skilled trade in a vocational-technical school setting. Thousands make a fine living as cosmetologists, electricians, automotive specialists, or in heating and air conditioning repair work.

Unless you're a highly driven entrepreneur or plan on learning a skilled trade in vocational-technical school, securing your college degree is a must. And your education won't stop there. Be prepared to be a lifelong learner by upgrading your skills and knowledge in continuing education classes and seminars.

9. TEMPORARIES, PART-TIMERS INCREASE

Once regarded as second-class job opportunities, temporaries and part-timers are emerging as respectable, even desirable, career steps—and for good reason. Surveys indicate that as many as 38 percent of temps worked their way back into a permanent position from one of their assignments.[14]

Some managers are hired back as consultants by the companies who laid them off. These contract executives are typically very task-oriented and very focused, and may be hired at a higher rate of pay than those who survived the cutbacks.

Some corporate cutbacks went too deep, or cuts were made in the wrong areas, leaving some departments understaffed. Indeed, estimates show that between one-third and one-half of the 1.4 million managers laid off in the early 1990s will return to their previous employer in one capacity or another.[15]

But managers are not the only people working temporary positions. Part-time jobs of less than 30 hours a week are growing. One reason: employers may pay as much as $4,000 a year just in health benefits to a full-time employee.[16] Additional costs for the employer come from vacation time, sick leave, holidays, and retirement benefits.

As a result, more American workers are holding down two or three jobs, making the United States surpass all other countries in the number of multiple jobholders.[17]

10. LIFE-LONG EDUCATION & UPGRADING OF SKILLS

Assuming that your current skills are sufficient for tomorrow's workplace may be an exercise in self-delusion. In the old work world, obtaining a college degree and finding one's niche in the company equalled job security. Workers engaged similar work processes and assignments for years at a time.

The attitude of "coasting" in your job, however, compares favorably to a pit stop during the Indianapolis 500 race. While you're parked in pit row, the rest of the field is racing by, leaving you in a constant "catch-up" posture.

In the new work environment, workers prepared for the 21st century must be in the constant mode of upgrading and refining their skills. Indeed, you are a steward of your natural strengths, talents, and skills. As such, God expects you to constantly be using and refining them.

In Matthew 25:14-30, Jesus taught the parable of the talents, understood as a measure of silver in the New Testament. Even though He was speaking of money, the principle of stewardship applies to the use of our natural talents from God. He blesses us when we invest our talents and use them for His glory. In fact, Jesus said, *"For everyone who has will be given more, and he will have an abundance. Whoever does not have, even what he has will be taken from him"* (Matthew 25:29).

Another way of stating this principle in modern language is "use it or lose it," meaning invest your talents or they will lose their value.

Christians should anticipate changes in the future work place with faith and courage. While it is impossible for us to predict precise details of the future, we do know the One who is already there. *"He will not let your foot slip—he who watches over you will not slumber.* (Psalm 121:3).

Your career pathway may not be easy or painless. But God's promise to you is that you will not walk it alone. He's with you each step of the way. ◆

ENDNOTES

1. "Today's Employment World," *Career Opportunity News,* Garrett Park Press, Vol. 12, No. 3, December, 1994: 1.

2. Dave Skidmore, Associated Press, "Threat of lay-off grows for some men," *Tallahassee Democrat,* May 13, 1994, sec. 1, page 3A.

3. James Medoff, "Why business is axing older workers," *U.S. News and World Report,* October 31, 1994: 78.

4. *Career Opportunity News,* p. 1.

5. Michael Kinsman, "Yesterday's jobs won't work tomorrow," *The Washington Times,* April 18, 1994, sec. 3: 3.

6. Frank Swoboda, "Reich Identifies 'Anxious Class' of Workers: Labor Day Speech Warns Work Force Needs More Education, Skills," *The Washington Post,* August 31, 1994, received through Compuserve.

7. "Information Technology, The Infobog, By the Numbers," *Fortune Magazine,* July 11, 1994, p. 62.

8. "Downsizing—the toll keeps going up," *U.S. News & World Report,* August 30 and September 6, 1993, p. 16.

9. *Career Opportunity News,* p. 3.

10. Norman M. Scarbrough and Thomas W. Zimmerer, "Entrepreneurs: The Driving Force Behind Small Business," *Effective Small Business Management* (NY: MacMillan), Fourth Edition, p. 4.

11. Lucie Young, "For More People, Home is Where the Work Is," *New York Times,* September 29, 1994, sec. B, p. 1.

12. *Career Opportunity News,* p. 5.

13. A. Gary Shilling, "Cutting Deals," *Forbes,* January 30, 1995, p. 142.

14. *Career Opportunity News,* p. 3.

15. Reuters, "Survivor Envy: When Managers Return as 'Advisors,' " *Investor's Business Daily,* September 20, 1993.

16. *Career Opportunity News,* p. 3.

17. Louise Uchitelle, "Moonlighting Plus: 3-Job Families on the Rise," *New York Times,* August 17, 1994, sec. A, p. 1.

7 Searching for a Job

As you begin your job search, there is no way to predict how it will go. Most likely it will require a focused and persistent effort on your part. Your attitude will be very important during this time, and the best way to have a good attitude is to keep the big picture in perspective. Ask yourself again: What is the purpose of my work? (See Chapter 3.)

Also, as discussed in Chapter 4, your job is to work the process diligently and allow God to bring about His results. Your job search will be a great opportunity to see how much you really trust God.

The job search is similar to a typical business or military operation. You identify your objective; you identify the resources needed to achieve your objective; and you develop a well thought-out strategy or plan. Of course, you should anticipate obstacles, and certainly you will have to adjust your plan as the unpredictable occurs.

Throughout your job search, you'll want to be open to God's leading in the process. Review Chapter 4 and pay special attention to the process chart on page 36.

Developing a Strategy for Job Search

It is important that you develop an overall strategy in your job search. Remember that you are marketing yourself to prospective employers, and any good marketing campaign must be based on a well-planned strategy.

The steps shown below outline a good strategy for working through the job search process.

Step 1. Determine Your Objective
Step 2. Develop Your Résumé
Step 3. Develop Your Reference Pool
Step 4. Network
Step 5. Respond to Classified Advertisements
Step 6. Consider Employment Agencies and Search Firms
Step 7. Consider Temporary Employment
Step 8. Consider Consulting

Step 9. Follow a Daily Schedule, Stay on Track, Keep Your Focus

Step 10. Conduct the Interview

Step 11. Negotiate the New Job

STEP 1 - DETERMINE YOUR OBJECTIVE (also refer to Chapters 2, 3, and 12 for further help).

Like a camera lens in focus, your objective should bring a range of compatible job possibilities into view. Taking the time to prayerfully do this can help you in at least two ways. a) A clear objective enables you to eliminate tempting jobs that are a mismatch. For instance, it's not uncommon for people to take a job they really don't like because it pays so well. Later, they regret the decision. b) A clear objective will help you to identify components of jobs that are consistent with your strengths.

Work through the following areas to help you solidify your objective.

Based on your career investigation, list the occupations for which you seem to be suited.

____________________ ____________________

____________________ ____________________

____________________ ____________________

What would be an ideal company for you to work for? (Describe what it would be like in terms of mission, organization, work activities, environment, processes, and values.)

Mission ______________________________

Organization __________________________

Work activities ________________________

Work environment _____________________

Processes ____________________________

Values ______________________________

By answering the previous questions, you should know what you are looking for and what you have to offer. Remember, employers are trying to fill a need. You are now in a position to accurately define your abilities to someone who may have a need you can fill.

Ideal Companies

List at least 5 companies that you feel meet all, or most of, the characteristics of the ideal company you've just described. Place a check (✓) before the names of the companies that totally qualify and an asterisk (*) before those that come close to qualifying. You will have to do some research to find out about companies. Check with the local Chamber of Commerce, the Department of Labor, and local colleges and technical schools. Your network of friends will be a help also.

1. ____
2. ____
3. ____
4. ____
5. ____

Now list 5 companies, or types of companies, for which you would *not* work—even if they offered you an appropriate job.

1. ____
2. ____
3. ____
4. ____
5. ____

Keep in mind that occasionally an organization will hire a quality person with high potential even without a clearly defined need. The Dallas Cowboys built a Super Bowl team in the 1970s by drafting the best athletes they could get and then working each one into a position.

▶ *STEP 2 - DEVELOP YOUR RÉSUMÉ (refer to Chapter 8)*

Target your résumé to focus on your objective. Decide which type of résumé best suits your situation.

▶ *STEP 3 - DEVELOP YOUR REFERENCE POOL*

You should compile a list of people who know something of your work history and are in a good position to evaluate your job performance. Select people who will feel comfortable speaking positively and specifically about you. Generally speaking, there are three types of people you should seriously consider as potential references:

a. Character references

b. Job performance references (preceding boss or high level colleague)

c. Professional expertise references (clients or competitors).

List several in each group who can be the most help; then contact them by phone. Discuss your situation and ask if they would be comfortable in giving you a good recommendation. You are getting permission to use their names and also getting a feel for how positively they feel about you. Refine your list to about two in each of the above categories.

Hints About References

- Have a good idea what your references will say.
- Be sure references know why you left your old job and what specific positions you are pursuing.
- Do not include references in your résumé.
- Have your reference list with you when you interview in case you need it.
- Remember to thank those who have agreed to be references; then thank them in writing after you get the job.

STEP 4 - NETWORK (Get the word out about you and the objective you are seeking. In doing so you will tap the hidden job market.)

The most effective method of finding a new job is through your contacts. The people you already know—your family, friends, business relations, and church family—are the most worthwhile and beneficial source of job leads because they know you and they know potential employers.

The vast majority of jobs are found through one form of personal contact or another.

As you identify your contacts, it is essential that you identify every individual who can possibly assist you in finding your next job.

Use the categories below to develop your network list. At this point, don't evaluate their ability to help you; just list names.

Network Categories

Use a separate page for each category and list names.

- Current or past employer
- Organizations where you have worked
- Customers and clients
- Vendors, service people, and suppliers
- Church
- College or educational institutions you have attended
- Social organizations or professional associations
- Other people you know looking for a job
- Family and friends
- Neighbors and community contacts
- Any other sources

Qualifying Your Contacts

Once you have completed your initial lists, you should review them to identify which contacts are:

- Likely to be the most valuable and productive,
- Sympathetic—will have a real interest in you,
- Easiest to contact,
- Better to postpone until later.

Now that you have qualified your contacts, determine what you want to accomplish when you talk with them. There are really four main goals you have when making a contact:

a. You may want to learn more about their industry, function, or career.

b. You may want to get other possible contacts from them, perhaps a direct contact to someone with hiring authority in their organization.

c. You may want to review your background and career goals with them to obtain their opinion about how you should proceed with your job search.

d. You may want to call for an interview.

All of these goals will allow you great flexibility in how you approach your network.

Considerations in Making Contacts

- Will the contact allow you to use his or her name?
- Will he or she make the initial phone call to someone else to set the stage for you?
- Should you call or write?
- What approach should you take when you call or write?
- If you phone, should you handle the questions you have over the phone or set up a face-to-face meeting?
- Is what you are asking within the person's ability to provide?

Using the Telephone to Network

Networking is most often done over the phone. It is especially effective because it eliminates unnecessary paperwork and provides immediate results. Phoning has the feel of informality, so many contacts will feel more at ease with you. Except for the phone call to get a direct interview, your typical approach to most contacts will be one of asking people to help you because of your respect for their experience and knowledge. The majority of people are flattered that you value their opinions and are more than happy to talk with you.

Tips on Phoning

Due to automated phone systems and voice mail, it may be difficult to get through. Be persistent and work smart. Be brief and give as little information as possible. Don't make the person uncomfortable or put them on the defensive. Follow up with a thank you note, no matter what the results. In fact, following up every contact will be one of the keys to a successful job search.

Networking via Letter

There are times, other than not being able to reach someone on the phone, that you may want to write rather than call. If you do, remember these guidelines:

- Do not include a résumé unless you have specifically been asked to do so by the person you are writing to.
- Ask for an appointment to discuss such things as career opportunities in the industry, future developments and direction, or some specific expertise you would like the person to share with you. Do not ask to talk about the possibility of employment.
- Briefly highlight three or four of your major accomplishments and/or credentials.
- Always mention the name of your referral, preferably in the first sentence of your letter.

PERSONAL CONTACT LETTER
(Phone follow-up)

1420 Glenview Rd
Brentwood, TN 37027

January 5, 199–

Mr. John Archer
Vice President, Marketing Division
Petro Oil, Inc.
147 Tacoma Pl
Toledo, OH 54321

Dear Mr. Archer: *(Use first name when possible)*

As you suggested during our telephone discussion yesterday, I am enclosing two copies of my résumé.

My goal is to become Project Manager of a medium-sized chemicals firm—preferably one that is involved in sulphur pollution problems. I have almost 20 years of experience in process design, cost, and on-site construction engineering. My work has taken me to numerous parts of the world and involved me in many types of processes, mostly in petrochemicals. I am interested in medium-sized companies in particular because I believe I can contribute more effectively to overall management where there is a real need for a broad-based generalist. At present, I prefer not to explore possibilities with consultants or contractors.

I have BSChemE and MSChemE degrees from the University of Tennessee and have taken accounting and organizational behavior courses in Vanderbilt's Owen MBA program. I have supervised as many as 50 people on recent $40–$80 million projects in Tennessee and Canada. I will relocate and travel if required.

I look forward to hearing from you if you have any suggestions along the lines I've described above.

Sincerely,

Ralph Brown

Enclosure

COMPANY CONTACT LETTER
(Direct approach)

Canflex American, Inc.
101 Broad St
Knoxville, TN 37425

December 7, 199–

Paula Bowman
Vice President, Advertising Division
Janes Electronics, Inc.
143 S 5th St
Nashville, TN 37210

Dear Ms. Bowman:

I am seeking a position as director of advertising and would appreciate exploring possibilities with your company. Mr. Francis McPhee of J. Walter Thompson, Inc. suggested I get in touch with you.

As my résumé indicates, I have 18 years of direct experience in advertising, promotion, and distribution. For six years, I was corporate director of advertising for Canflex America, a $20 million consumer hi-fi manufacturer. In carrying out those responsibilities, I built a successful organization and a record of significant achievement.

As you may know, Canflex has recently been acquired and its advertising function shifted to the parent company. My goal, therefore, is to join a small to medium-sized organization such as yours, where I can even more actively participate in key policy-making decisions.

I have an MBA in marketing from Columbia University. I wish to stay in the mid-south area of the country; however, travel poses no problem for me.

I will call you in a week or so to discuss whatever opportunities there may be with your company or any suggestions you may have regarding possibilities with other organizations. If you would like to contact me, please call me either at Canflex (615) 555-0004 or at my residence (615) 555-2102. Thank you for your consideration.

Sincerely,

Roger C. Williams

Enclosure

COMPANY CONTACT LETTER
(Indirect approach)

September 11, 199–

Mr. John A. Davidson
Executive Vice President, Operations
Krypton Art Manufacturing Company
43901 Verde Blvd
Greenleaf, MN 10532

Dear Mr. Davidson:

Although we're not personally acquainted, perhaps you could take a few moments to help me with my information search.

I have been an internal consulting engineer for large corporations in the area of process engineering for the past 20 years. I plan on leaving my present employer and am seeking a new position with an organization in which I can apply my broad range of skills to productivity improvement programs.

While I realize there may be no openings in your firm at this time, I thought you might know of other people or organizations who would be interested in someone whose background and achievements (as shown in my résumé) uniquely blend practical problem-solving, creativity, and integrated concept engineering. These are a potent combination for producing results in high technology and/or high volume production settings.

I think you will agree that the best way to find a new position in the "hidden job market" is through word of mouth, and I am hoping you can provide me with some suggestions. May I count on your help? I will call in a week or so to answer any questions you may have, as well as to obtain any leads you would be kind enough to suggest. Once again, thanks for your assistance.

Very truly yours,

Joseph B. Keating

Enclosure

▶ *STEP 5 - RESPOND TO CLASSIFIED ADVERTISEMENTS*

Although many companies place advertisements in major newspapers and elsewhere in their recruiting efforts, you should be aware that only 10 percent to 15 percent of positions available are advertised.

There are two types of company-paid ads: "open" and "blind." An "open" ad lists not only the qualifications an individual employer is looking for and what he or she is prepared to offer the right candidate, but it also includes the name and address of that company (and sometimes even the particular person to whom you should write and send your résumé). The advantage of an "open" ad is that it affords you the opportunity of researching the company thoroughly and/or making discreet inquiries about the job itself through knowledgeable personal contacts. This, in turn, can help you considerably in writing the cover letter that will accompany your résumé and in tailoring it as closely as possible to the company's requirements.

"Blind" ads, on the other hand, do not include the name of the company; instead, responses to them are forwarded by means of a newspaper box number that appears at the end of each ad. Such advertisements make your task more difficult because you really are not able to "customize" the letter you send to the company. Furthermore, there is the very strong likelihood that receipt of your letter may not even be acknowledged.

Where to Look for Advertisements

Classified sections of weekend newspapers, in *National Business Employment Weekly,* in ad services that can be found at local library, or in trade and professional journals.

Helpful Hints

Be sure to read each advertisement attentively. Try to extract as much information, implicit as well as explicit, as you possibly can. An advertisement costs a company quite a bit of money, so you should weigh each word it contains. Remember, your goal is to "decipher" the message so that you are assured of being on target when you respond to it.

Whether the ad calls for it or not, always include a cover letter with a copy of your résumé.

Even if the ad explicitly states that you should indicate the salary you expect to receive, probably the best thing to do is to skirt this issue. The proper place to discuss the question of salary is at the interview itself. When salary history is requested, be aware that some employers will screen out those candidates that do not include it. You must make a personal determination to include it or not.

STEP 6 - CONSIDER EMPLOYMENT AGENCIES AND SEARCH FIRMS

Both search firms and employment agencies tend to specialize in certain kinds of jobs, such as engineering, finance, marketing, or production. Employment agencies seldom place "box number" ads in newspapers, since they are the kinds of organizations that benefit significantly from high visibility. On the other hand, search firms more often will use "blind ads." Employment agencies and search firms represent the corporations/businesses, not the job seekers.

In most states, agencies are regulated and are not allowed to charge clients for placement or they are not allowed to charge until after placement. Avoid those with up-front fees.

Search firms are commissioned to fill specific needs of a company—generally limited to higher salary levels.

It is important to know something about the agency or search firm you are dealing with.

- What types of jobs do they specialize in?
- Who are some of the clients?
- Are they also a temporary agency?
- Do they have references? Who are some people they have placed that you can talk with?
- Who pays for their services?

If at all possible, meet the people you are talking with. Some agencies tend to "push paper"—meaning the more résumés they send out the greater their chances of placing someone. Be aware that your résumé could end up anywhere.

► *STEP 7 - CONSIDER TEMPORARY EMPLOYMENT*

One of the fastest growing new concepts in America today is that of temporary employment services. Temporary employment agencies are springing up in every city and are providing a good service to both employer and the unemployed.

The employer benefits by having someone to fill a need that may or may not become permanent. Employers also use temporaries to fill a void while they conduct a thorough search for a replacement. They also use temporaries to fill seasonal needs or to fill vacancies during growth spurts. Using a temporary can be a good way to try out new employees before committing to them.

Many temporary employees become full-time employees. You should consider temporary employment as a way to pay your bills and as a way to get your foot in the door to show your capabilities.

► *STEP 8 - CONSIDER CONSULTING*

Do you have expertise in some areas in which you could be a part-time consultant? If so, you should make some contacts to see if others might be interested in using your services.

Consultants are becoming a very popular way for companies to fill specific and limited needs without hiring a full-time employee. Consulting has become a practical and fulfilling career for many who have become unemployed in recent years. Research the pros and cons thoroughly and be sure to read Chapter 10 on "Starting a Business" before you make a decision to become a consultant.

STEP 9 - FOLLOW A DAILY SCHEDULE, STAY ON TRACK, KEEP YOUR FOCUS

If you are unemployed, your job search is your work. Set goals and deadlines for carrying out your strategy. Make yourself accountable by using deadlines. Develop a written work schedule. Spend six to eight hours per day looking for work. Then relax, read, and relate to family members. Get a good nights sleep. Take care of yourself physically: eat normally and exercise regularly.

Seek godly counsel: someone to share ideas on job search, someone to encourage you when you are down, someone to hold you accountable—prod you to stay on schedule in your job search.

Keep focused:

- Expect difficulties and discouragement (see Chapter 11).
- Trust God (see Chapter 4).

STEP 10 - CONDUCT THE INTERVIEW

This is a critical step in securing your new job and, as a result, we've devoted Chapter 9 to this topic.

STEP 11 - NEGOTIATE THE NEW JOB

When you are offered a job, the tendency is to go sky high. That's normal, but be sure to keep your feet on the ground and listen carefully to what is said. You need to know exactly what is offered. If you have questions, be sure to ask for clarification. Many people view job negotiations simply as a matter of coming to terms with an employer on the question of salary. This is not the case at all. A number of other important factors should be discussed and possibly negotiated.

- Starting date
- Vacations
- Decision-making authority
- Support, budget, and resources
- Reporting relationships
- Relocation and its expenses
- Insurance and pension benefits
- Employment contracts
- Release time for professional memberships and activity
- Stock options
- Bonus arrangements
- Title

Though it is highly unlikely you will be able to negotiate successfully on *all* of the above items, the extent to which you can maneuver is generally determined by the nature and level of the job and by the hiring policies of that company. Remember also that any negotiating you have in mind should be opened only after an agreement has been reached (at least in principle) that you will be joining the organization.

The key to successful negotiations is knowing exactly what you want from the potential employer. Don't surrender anything until you have to and, then, only if it is *not* one of your top priorities. If possible, get the employer to make an initial offer. Once he or she has done this, you can suggest whatever modifications you feel are important or anything else that will make the offer more palatable or attractive to you.

Finally, remember that it never hurts just to ask for something. God's Word says, *"You do not have, because you do not ask God. When you ask, you do not receive, because you ask with wrong motives, that you may spend what you get on your pleasures"* (James 4:2-3). Your natural urgency to get the job shouldn't prevent you from trying to attain a benefit to which you're legitimately entitled and that you'd be unhappy *not* to have, once you actually start working.

SOME ADDITIONAL HINTS

Obtaining the top dollar for one's services is not an easy matter and requires some finely honed negotiating skills. Keep your discussions of money on an impersonal level, and be as business-like, dispassionate, and logical as you can.

If you have genuine conviction that you're worth the money you are asking for, your voice and manner will reflect this fact. By itself, this by no means guarantees you'll get the desired salary; however, it will improve your general bargaining position.

Since most large companies have a more or less preset salary structure for positions, there usually is not too much room for maneuvering. Nonetheless, you should seek the level that is appropriate for your situation. (If you don't know what the salary scale is, ask.) You should be prepared to explore such key fringe benefits as *stock options.*

As crucial as salary is, there are other considerations that are equally important, if not more so. These include—especially for senior executives—matters such as scope of responsibility, degree of autonomy, and the challenge the job offers. Don't ignore or underrate them!

One of the headiest experiences a person can have is to be warmly courted for a desirable job. Obviously, there is a real temptation to jump at such an offer, particularly if it represents a significant salary increase. Experience has shown, though, that a certain amount of restraint on your part (not to be confused with lack of enthusiasm) will pay off in the long run. Remember, it is the Lord God you are serving. Pray for humility during your negotiations.

CLOSING THE DEAL

Now that you are so close to having made your job campaign a successful one, it is very important that you do nothing that might jeopardize your chances. This is *not* the time to take foolish risks or relax your efforts. Too many "sure things" have been known to slip away at the very last minute simply because they were taken for granted.

Here, then, are some final words of caution and ways to be self-protective:

- Agree on a decision date—and be sure to give your answer by that date.
- Don't cut off other options until you have actually started working. Until you're on the payroll, you don't have anything more than the employer's word.
- If possible, try to get the employer to "put it in writing."
- Be certain that no "contingencies" remain in the air. For example, have all reference and security checks been made? Have you passed the medical exam?
- Don't trumpet it about—to anyone—that you've found new employment until it is truly a closed deal. Premature celebrations have a funny way of backfiring.
- Once you've started on your new job, remember to write or call the other people with whom you were negotiating, to thank them for their time and interest in you.
- Don't forget to thank the many individuals who were instrumental in helping you during your job search. They have done you a great service.

A TIME FOR GRATITUDE

Once all the negotiations are completed and you are "officially" with the company, it is appropriate to give thanks to God. We are to be as earnest in thanksgiving to God as we were when seeking His wisdom and direction in the job search. After all, it is very easy to forget or slip into taking credit for what God has accomplished for us.

Moses knew Israel would be tempted to do just that. For that reason, he offered terse counsel to the nation prior to their entrance into the Promised Land. While his entire admonition is found in Deuteronomy 8:11-20, we are including just a portion here.

"Be careful that you do not forget the Lord your God, failing to observe his commands, his laws and his decrees that I am giving you this day. Otherwise, when you eat and are satisfied, when you build fine houses and settle down, and when your herds and flocks grow large and your silver and gold increase and all you have is multiplied, then your heart will become proud and you will forget the Lord your God, who brought you out of Egypt, out of the land of slavery.

"You may say to yourself, 'My power and the strength of my hands have produced this wealth for me.' But remember the Lord your God, for it is he who gives you the ability to produce wealth, and so confirms his covenant, which he swore to your forefathers, as it is today" (Deuteronomy 8:11-14, 17-18).

With the new job in hand, you have a wonderful testimony to offer to all who will listen. Be sure your family, especially children, understand God's role in supplying your needs. Being hired in a new job provides a golden opportunity to teach and illustrate God's principles.

You also will have a powerful word of encouragement to those still searching for employment or who are yet unhappy in their work. Give credit to the Lord. Someone may even accept salvation because of your testimony.

You may want to honor God by inviting your intercessory prayer partners, family, friends, and neighbors into your home for a festive celebration in His honor. ◆

“In order to write a good résumé, you must have a clear grasp of what your purpose is, who the recipients will be, and how they will view it. A well-written résumé provides hard-hitting evidence that will convince the reader that you’re well equipped to master the new job.”

Lee Ellis
Director, Career Pathways

8 Writing a Résumé

A résumé provides a well-thought-out, concise picture of you—the job seeker. It must communicate quickly, clearly, and accurately your objective, qualifications, experience, and accomplishments. The résumé is usually a first impression of you and, therefore, is a very important piece of paper.

Most people don't like to write about themselves, so we strongly encourage you to get some help with your résumé. Your spouse, parents, or a knowledgeable friend might be able to provide assistance. Also, someone who reviews résumés in the course of his or her job could provide good insights. Finally, consider professional help but, as we have cautioned, check them out first.

We hope this chapter will provide you a sufficient foundation so you'll be able to develop your own résumé, with a little critique from a friend or coach. The encouragement you get should help you through the stress of the résumé process.

Your Sales Brochure

Your résumé is an extremely important document. It is your personal sales brochure. Remember the following:

- *You* are the product the résumé is trying to sell.
- Résumés are designed to allow many people to get to know you quickly and easily during the course of your job search.
- Your résumé must be high quality—both in content and in appearance. Be sure it looks good!
- Nobody likes to feel that, in effect, he or she is being reduced to a mere scrap of paper, but you have little choice if you want a job.
- Just as in sales brochures, you must highlight the key benefits of the product (you).
- Résumés are used at every level of the organizational world.

There may be times when you will need more than one résumé; for example, if you want to stress tasks and achievements that will be of special interest to a particular employer. Such a résumé could give you a competitive edge by demonstrating that you are the right candidate for a specific job. On the other hand, don't spend your valuable time rewriting résumés when you actually should be involved in a job search. Most of the time you can use a résumé cover letter to clarify how well suited you are to a particular field.

Writing Your Résumé

- No one can write a top-notch résumé on the first try; you will need to make several rough drafts.
- Your first draft should be as long as necessary to include all the facts you think are important and relevant.
- Revise and edit it until you have tailored your résumé to the desired length.
- Ideally, you should end up with a one- or two-page résumé. Employers and search firms simply don't have the time or the patience to deal with too lengthy a document.
- Your résumé must do its job in the first five to twenty seconds. That is the time you have to "catch the eye" of the decision maker. Though that may not seem fair, it is realistic.
- Your résumé should avoid being so slick that it comes across as being phony. Anyone whose job is to read and evaluate résumés knows that often they are prepared by professionals.
- The most important thing in your résumé is the information, not the fancy print or paper.
- As one of your key sales tools, your résumé should do the following.
  1. Identify the main features of the product (you).
  2. Emphasize your special skills.
  3. Highlight your achievements and the end result of your activities.
  4. Indicate the techniques and processes you are an expert at implementing.
- Your future employer needs to know your potential, so don't downplay your achievements. If humility prevents this, ask someone who knows you well to help you communicate the impact of your work.

- Don't get hung up on describing your job duties and/or your other credentials so literally that you forget about what the prospective employer really wants to know: namely, ample evidence of your capacity to handle the particular job you are applying for.
- A résumé is a form of written communication, and all communication is a two-way street.
  1. Focus on the message you're trying to convey.
  2. As you review your résumé, put yourself in the place of the person who will read it.
  3. Ask yourself: "If I were the employer, would I have a very clear understanding of the job candidate being presented here?" Unless your answer is a solid "yes," you still have some work to do.
- Your résumé is your calling card; you want it to make the best possible impression on the person who receives it. Toward this end, take the time and effort needed for putting your best foot forward.
- Your résumé should be well designed, informative, and consistently formatted.
- Your résumé should be airy looking. No one wants to read huge blocks of solid type.

Even though a well-prepared résumé is important, it does not get you a job; it gets you an interview. *You* get the job!

Pitfalls to Avoid in Résumé Design

• *Devoting more space to early jobs than to more recent ones.*

• *Overemphasizing your educational background.* If you have been out of school for five years or more, your résumé should reflect that fact by being weighted in the direction of your *work* experience.

• *Leaving gaps between employment dates.* Avoid the appearance of any time gaps between jobs. You can accomplish this in two ways.

1. Give a reason for being temporarily unemployed. For example, returning to school full time for additional training, traveling, or military service.
2. List your jobs by the year you were employed rather than by the month and year. For example, instead of ending one job "June 1978" and beginning the next one with "February 1979," omit the months, list only the years, and eliminate the appearance of a time gap.

In the event the actual gap is more substantial than this example, or if you've held several jobs in quick succession, it may be best to omit dates altogether and use a *Functional Skills Résumé* as discussed below.

3. Avoid being too lengthy. Your résumé is not a career obituary!

Avoid procrastinating or being so picky that you never finish your résumé. Concentrate your efforts and get done quickly.

Types of Résumés

There are two primary formats for résumés that we recommend: reverse chronological and functional. (Examples of both are shown at the end of this chapter.) You can have small variations in these, depending on the unique situation of the individual. Generally it is better to stick fairly close to these formats because they are what employers are accustomed to seeing. On the other hand, your goal in writing the résumé is to present yourself as a unique person with special gifts to offer the company.

A. **Reverse Chronological Format.** (See Example #1 on page 88.) This format highlights your jobs and what you did in them. It is especially good for showing a progression of responsibility as in Example #1. This résumé format might be preferred if you are staying in the same career field, where the job progression will have more relevance.

   Remember that the chronological résumé format is not just a laundry list of when and where you worked. The jobs should come alive and highlight the impact you had on the organization. Avoid using more space for old jobs than for recent ones.

B. **Functional Skills Résumé.** If you have not had an outstanding job progression, you have little experience, or you are changing career fields, you might want to consider this format. It will focus on the strengths you have to offer the company.

   In the functional résumé you will use headings that focus on the skills you have that would apply to the specific job you are seeking. Use bullet statements to highlight your experience and lend impact to the organizations. A bullet statement is simply an action-oriented statement that describes how you used or developed a skill in the past. By using bullets you can highlight the appropriate attributes you have to offer the employer.

   As you can see in Example #2 (page 90), the individual was changing career fields and wanted to highlight his education and newly acquired skills, rather than his previous

Air Force jobs. In Example #3 (page 92), the individual had some job experience, yet gained a stronger presentation of her abilities by using the functional format. Examples #4 and #5 on page 93 and 94 also use functional format résumés.

Because this format emphasizes skills, employers and employment dates are downplayed and often are shown toward the end of the document.

What to Include in Your Résumé

The best way to develop your résumé is to look at some good models and then adapt them to your specific situation. We've included several résumés for your use as examples of what to include.

Remember that you want to highlight your strong points and, therefore, may want to make subtle adjustments to the format to suit your situation. For instance, the résumés in Examples #2 and #5 present education before skills and experience, but Examples #3 and #4 show education near the end. The best résumés paint a picture of a unique person.

The bottom line for your résumé: Be honest, show your impact in the workplace, and make it look professional.

What to Leave Out of Your Résumé

- Specific names of **references** (This should be reserved for the interview.)
- Reasons for **leaving** a previous position (This also should be dealt with during the interview.)
- Your present **salary**
- **Outside activities** which are not relevant to the job (In some cases, you may want to include church or clubs, but use discretion.)
- Dramatic or fancy **type or styling** (in fact anything that might be considered eccentric)
- Colored résumé **paper** (use white, gray, or cream/buff bond)
- **Personal data**—age, marital status, number of children, health conditions
- **Typographical, spelling, or grammatical errors**—These can quickly eliminate you from consideration; proofread carefully.

Sample Achievement Statements

The general appearance of your résumé (neatness, accuracy, organization) gives the first impression of you. Once the reader gets into your work experience, it is the impact of your accomplishments that attracts attention. You want to use strong verbs and verifiable facts as much as possible.

The following are some examples of how to describe achievements.

- Perfect attendance at work for last three years (1992-1995) while maintaining a 96 percent on-time delivery rate with EPS Overnight Delivery.
- Provided expert lawn care to four businesses, two apartment complexes, and nine residences for three years. Business increased 50 percent during that period; never lost a customer.
- Planned, organized, and supervised all activities for a banquet of 300 people.
- Raised $20,000 for the Gainesville Care Home.
- Managed and maintained medical records of 1200 patients for two doctors; received bonus and letter of recognition five years successively for superior performance.
- Increased regional sales by 12 percent, resulting in an increase of $42,000 net profit.
- Developed and conducted financial training seminars for 18 small businesses and non-profit organizations.
- Selected as "Employee of the Year."
- Wrote operations manual which is used by over 2,000 employees in three company plants.
- Established and implemented all personnel policies and procedures to include recruiting, hiring, evaluation, and benefits for an organization of 160 people.
- Opened and developed four accounts which generated $420,000 in annual sales.
- Developed personal computer spreadsheets, pricing forms, and quarterly account sales reviews.
- Typing speed 60 wpm; highly proficient in Lotus, Dbase IV, and WordPerfect.
- Deployed and led a team of eight logistic technicians in providing on-time supplies to 4,000 soldiers (31st Regiment) during Operation Desert Storm.

A FEW FINAL HINTS

- Most people use short phrases, rather than complete sentences, when writing their résumés. But, whichever you employ, be sure you are consistent; in other words, don't shift indiscriminately from one form to the other.
- Don't abbreviate. The reader may not understand.
- Spell out all numerals up to and including the number "nine." Use the numerical form for "10" and above.
- Highlight certain items to make them stand out by using capital letters, dashes, underlining, italics, or "bullets." A good general rule, though, is to use them discreetly; overusing them will have a counterproductive effect.
- Wherever possible, use the *present* tense in describing your current job (manage rather than managed). However, if you are describing something already implemented or achieved, you'll obviously want to use the past tense.
- Squeeze out all the excess prose. If you can say something in three words, don't use 10.
- Try to design your résumé in such a way that you don't begin a description on the first page and continue it on the next page.
- An employer should be able to read your résumé at a glance. Careful design and clearly marked headings will achieve this goal.

Your Résumé Checklist

1. **Categories**

   Name, address, phone number(s)

   Objective

   Summary (optional)

   Professional experience or skills

   - Dates
   - Company name
   - Job title
   - Job description
     - responsibilities
     - duties
     - achievements

Education

Name of institution

Degree(s)

Year(s)

Other

Professional memberships

Awards

Honors

Publications

2. Format

Logically organized

Reverse chronology (where applicable)

Internal consistency

Appropriate amount of space for each entry

3. Layout

Margins

external

internal

Airiness

Easy readability

Eye-catching (underlining and use of capitalization)

Individualized (has a "personal touch")

4. General

Avoidance of abbreviations

Inclusion of exact detail

Sentences versus phrases (consistent use of one or the other)

Achievement-oriented

5. Proofreading

Spelling

Punctuation

Written style

corrections

naturalness

clarity

absence of clichés or business jargon

Effective Sentence Openers

People who read and evaluate résumés are interested in *results*, rather than activities. So, be alert for any job description that does not indicate precisely what you have *achieved.*

One way to be sure that you are seen as the person *responsible* for the achievements you claim is to use strong, direct, and positive-sounding verbs as sentence openers. (A list of such verbs is provided below.) At the same time, refrain from employing verbs or verbal phrases that suggest either vagueness, partial responsibility, or else a passive approach to the duties being described (was responsible for, worked on, was a member of, studied, analyzed, reviewed).

accomplished
accelerated
achieved
activated
added
administrated
advanced
approved
assigned
assisted
chose
completed
conceived
conducted
consolidated
controlled
coordinated
created
decreased
delivered
demonstrated
designed
developed
devised
directed
doubled
eliminated
established
exceeded
excelled
expanded
fabricated
formulated
guided
generated
hired
identified
implemented
improved
increased
initiated
installed
introduced
joined
launched
led
maintained
managed
modified
negotiated
obtained
organized
originated
overhauled
participated
performed
planned
processed
programmed
promoted
proposed
purchased
recommended
recruited
redesigned
reduced
renovated
reorganized
replaced
researched
revamped
saved
scheduled
serviced
simplified
skilled
sold
solved
spearheaded
stabilized
standardized
started
streamlined
strengthened
stretched
structured
succeeded
summarized
superseded
supervised
surveyed
systematized
terminated
tested
trained
transacted
transferred
translated
tripled
trimmed
turned
uncovered
unified
unraveled
widened
won
withdrew
wrote

Résumé Work Sheet

(Use worksheets like this to organize your work history. Then condense into impact statements for your résumé.)

EXPERIENCE

Company name ______________________________________

Location ____

Dates of employment _________________________________

Title ____

Overview of position _________________________________

Accomplishments (Highlight the skills you want to use in your next job.) ____

Company name ______________________________________

Location ____

Dates of employment _________________________________

Title ____

Overview of position _________________________________

Accomplishments (Highlight the skills you want to use in your next job.) ____

Sample Résumé Cover Letter

234 Columns Dr
Athens, GA 00089
April 15, 1995

Mr. William Johnson, Manager
Toga Men's Wear
2000 Shopping Dr
Athens, GA 00090

Dear Mr. Johnson:

I am writing to request consideration for employment with your company. Although young in age, I have demonstrated the ability to handle considerable responsibility. In addition, I have developed job skills that would enable me to be a successful sales representative for your company.

I am also interested in working for your firm because of your reputation in the community for helping college students who are working their way through school. I have been accepted at the University of Georgia, where I plan to study finance and marketing. I am highly motivated and believe I could be both a good student and a good employee for your firm.

As you can see from the enclosed résumé, my achievements at school, at work, and in extracurricular activities have prepared me well for a position with your company. I would be happy to provide references at your request.

I will call you during the week of April 21-25 to see if we can schedule an appointment. Thank you for your time and for considering my résumé and possible employment with your company.

Very sincerely yours,

Jim Wilson

Enclosure

EXAMPLE #1

(Reverse Chronological Format)

James P. Smith
487 Cypress Lane
Yorba Linda, CA 92686
(512) 555-1010

OBJECTIVE

Responsibilities in administration—finance or operations—of a sound, growing financial institution or service company.

EMPLOYMENT HISTORY

Union Savings Association, Yorba Linda, California 1983–1995
Medium sized thrift with nine locations.

President-Chief Executive Officer 1995

Senior Vice President-Chief Financial Officer 1995

Supervision of accounting, treasury, human resources and information resource management.

Senior Vice President-Information Resource Management and Human Resources 1989-1995

Responsible for all computer resources and all personnel/payroll functions.

- Coordinated two investigations of alternative mainframe systems, resulting in a decision to change processors.
- Coordinated the design and installation of in-house item processing system, ATM system and general ledger system.
- Selected, installed, and managed a local area network of microcomputers serving 18 workstations.
- Designed and implemented a corporate records management system including the physical facility and computerization.

Also served in the following capacities as a senior officer:

- Member of Senior Officer Committee, Chairman of Information Resource Management Steering Committee, Employee Involvement Committee, and Employee Stock Ownership Plan Committee.
- Responsible for all corporate insurance—evaluation, purchases, and claims.
- Designated liaison with state and federal regulators during examinations, and with all potential acquirors of the Association.
- Managed sale and liquidation of two wholly owned subsidiaries: an insurance agency and a lease financing company.
- Participated in or chaired task forces to:
  1. Improve the quality of customer service,
  2. Design a formal structure for evaluating and compensating employees,
  3. Work out recurring problems with negotiable items, and
  4. Solicit proxies from stockholders for a tender offer for the Association's stock.

Senior Vice President-Chief Financial Officer 1985–1989

Vice President-Controller 1983–1985

Swift, Bridges and Company, Wilmington, Texas 1980–1983
Regional accounting firm serving Texas and New Mexico.

Audit Manager
Complete engagement responsibility for all financial institution audits.

- Partner-level responsibilities in audit quality control program.
- Instructor for local office training programs.

Michael Drefuss & Co., Oakland Texas 1976-1980
International accounting firm

Audit Manager 1979-1980
Full engagement responsibility for banks, savings and loan associations, a commercial finance company and a regulated investment company.

- Served as Firm's primary liaison with thrift executives in North Texas through involvement in industry organizations.

Audit Senior 1978-1979

Audit Staff 1976-1977

EDUCATION AND AFFILIATIONS

Stevens College, Abilene, Texas 1970
Bachelor of Business Administration

Certified Public Accountant, licensed in Texas 1971

East Point Chapel, Wilmington, Texas 1971
Treasurer and member of Finance Committee 1989–1995

Christian Financial Concepts, Gainesville, Georgia 1989-1995
Seminar leader and counselor in personal financial management

- REFERENCES AVAILABLE UPON REQUEST -

EXAMPLE #2 (Functional Skills Format)

JAMES M. ODEN
324 Broad St
Monroe, Georgia 30655
(706) 555-1212

Objective: Position as a counselor in a career development setting, helping clients evaluate their interests, abilities/disabilities, and deal with personal, social, academic, and occupational problems.

HIGHLIGHTS OF QUALIFICATIONS

- Completion of intensive counseling practicum with a variety of clients.
- Graduated with honors from all studies while working full time.
- Certified occupational education teacher.
- Ability to inspire respect, trust, and confidence.
- Sincere compassion; able to empathize with a diversity of people.

RELEVANT SKILLS AND EXPERIENCE

Individual Counseling

- Counseled clients, of all backgrounds and ages, on a wide range of issues: Family and peer relationships; Drug and alcohol abuse; Test anxiety; Abuse/neglect; Stress; Workplace problems

Testing and Evaluation

- Trained and experienced in test design and construction, administration, and data correlation.
- Administered and interpreted a full range of instruments, including: Myers-Briggs Type Indicator; Armed Services Vocational Aptitude Battery; Career Occupational Preference System; Strong Campbell Interest Inventory

Group Counseling

- Facilitated adolescent and adult groups concerning: Coping skills; Vocational development; Interpersonal relationships; Academic deficiencies

Career Development

- Experienced in the use of computer programs for student college search and career decision making.
- Counseled individuals on life/career goal setting; Career information research; Employee transition outplacement

EDUCATION

Masters Degree in Counseling (grade average 3.97/4.0), 1994, UNIVERSITY OF PHOENIX, Phoenix AZ

Bachelors Degree in Vocational Education /Corporate Training and Development (grade average 3.72/4.0), 1992, WAYLAND BAPTIST UNIVERSITY, Plainview TX

Associate Degree in Instructional Technology, 1990, COMMUNITY COLLEGE OF THE AIR FORCE, Montgomery AL

Computer Literacy

- Trained and experienced in the use of software applications: Word processing; Spreadsheets; Databases; Statistical analysis; Educational programs

EMPLOYMENT HISTORY

1988–92 **Community College of the Air Force Faculty Instructor/ Instructor-Trainer** -
SHEPPARD AIR FORCE BASE, Wichita Falls TX

1987–88 **Administrator of Hospital Dental Service** -
MYRTLE BEACH AIR FORCE BASE SC

1985–87 **Dental Hygienist/Oral Surgeon Technician/Training Supervisor** -
MYRTLE BEACH AIR FORCE BASE SC

1985–87 **Emergency Medical Technician** -
MYRTLE BEACH RESCUE SQUAD, Myrtle Beach SC

1984–85 **Dental Assisting and Radiological Specialist** -
MYRTLE BEACH AIR FORCE BASE SC

1984 **Men's Clothing Selling Specialist** -
J.C. PENNEY COMPANY, Bogart GA

1983 **Construction Worker** -
FLATBED NUCLEAR GENERATING STATION, Ottawa KS

HONORS

National Defense Service Medal
National Dean's List of American Universities and Colleges
Master Instructor Certification
Air Force Commendation Medal
Outstanding Medical Airman of the Year

PROFESSIONAL AFFILIATIONS

- American College Personnel Association (ACPA)
- Career Planning and Adult Development Network
- National Career Development Association (NCDA)
- National Employment Counselors Association (NECA)
- Military Educators and Counselors Association (MECA)

- REFERENCES AVAILABLE UPON REQUEST -

EXAMPLE #3

(Functional Skills Format)

JANE A. SMITH
4110 DOGWOOD ST
CORNELIA, GEORGIA 30531
(404) 555-1919

OBJECTIVE: Writing/editing position, with opportunity to work with desktop publishing systems

HIGHLIGHTS OF QUALIFICATIONS

* Over three years experience in the publishing field
* Reputation for accuracy in writing and editing
* Skilled in research and organization of written articles
* Highly conscientious worker with experience in meeting deadlines while maintaining quality

REVELANT SKILLS AND EXPERIENCE

Write/Edit/Proofread

- Organized, developed and wrote factual articles for three well-respected regional food industry publications
- Edited news releases and other submitted materials to a suitable size
- Proofread copy for publications
- Collaborated with production manager in making sure advertisements were produced to specifications, ensuring client satisfaction
- Completed proofreading workshop sponsored by Superior Builders, 1989

Research/Interview

- Conducted research for articles utilizing various print media
- Interviewed food industry executives both by telephone and in person as part of research for articles

Computer Operation

- Over three years experience on IBM personal computer, utilizing WordStar and MicroSoft Word word processing systems
- Trained on Macintosh Quark Xpress desktop publishing software system

EMPLOYMENT HISTORY

March-June 1992—Associate Editor
August 1988-February 1992—Business Writer/Reporter
Detail Wrightsville Publishing Company, Inc.
Wrightsville, GA

1985, 86, 87 Summer Day Camp Counselor
Wrightsville Parks and Recreation Dept.
Wrightsville, GA

EDUCATION

A.B., English, University of Georgia, Athens, 1988. Summa cum laude, Phi Beta Kappa
A.A., Gainesville College, Gainesville, Georgia, 1986. Dean's List

- REFERENCES AVAILABLE UPON REQUEST -

EXAMPLE #4

(Functional Skills Format)

KATHERINE A. WILSON
1000 CHATTAHOOCHEE RD
GAINESVILLE, GA 30503
(404) 503-4951

Objective: Position in Administrative Services, with an opportunity for personal growth and career development.

HIGHLIGHTS OF ABILITIES

* Highly organized and detail oriented
* Excellent communication skills
* Supportive team worker; committed and responsible
* Reliable and adaptable; learn new processes quickly; and take initiative

RELEVANT SKILLS AND EXPERIENCE

Office Experience

* Maintained folders and information for over 5,000 clients.
* Operated a wide range of office machines, including:
  -copiers, printers, typewriters, voice mail
* Processed incoming and outgoing mail.

Telephone and Communication Skills

* Managed inbound and outbound call activities to include:
  -customer service
  -customer and home office correspondence
* Explained insurance policies to clients.

Computer Knowledge

* Operate various software applications: word processing, databases, statistical testing analysis. (IBM compatible)
* Process and scan test packages daily.

EMPLOYMENT HISTORY

Present	Administrative Assistant	Mountainview Nursing Home, Gainesville, GA
1991-92	Administrative Assistant	World Insurance, Athens, GA
1991	Scoring Technician	Career Pathways, Gainesville, GA
*1989-91	Waitress/Event Organizer	Columns Country Club, Athens, GA
*1988	Packaging/Customer Assistance	Bigg's Grocery Store, Athens, GA
*1987-88	Children's Clothing Specialist	Mall Dept. Store, Athens, GA
*1986-87	Banquet Waitress	University of Georgia, Athens, GA
*1986	Cashier	Flavers Dept. Store, Athens, GA

*Part-time jobs held during high school/college

EDUCATION

North Georgia College, Dahlonega, GA 1988-89, Psychology Major.

- REFERENCES AVAILABLE UPON REQUEST -

EXAMPLE #5 **(Modified Functional Skills Format)**

James T. Wilson
234 Columns Dr
Athens, GA 00089

OBJECTIVE: A part-time position in sales or customer support. Desire to build an employment relationship that will continue throughout four years as a college student.

SUMMARY: A confident, outgoing individual who enjoys meeting people and presenting products or ideas. Personal strengths include:

Enjoy selling, results-oriented

Energetic with strong initiative

Strong verbal skills

Enjoy meeting people

Dependable, seek responsibility

WORK EXPERIENCE:

Customer Assistance/Stocker, 1990-1992. Sky-Mart, Commerce, Georgia. Fourteen hours per week. Outstanding attendance record. Started at bottom and moved up to weekend supervisor of sporting goods and auto accessories. Paid cash for first auto from earnings.

Lawn Care, 1988-1990. Self-employed lawn business. Began with three customers and increased to nine. Gained experience in promotion, financial management, and customer relations. Never lost a customer. Saved $1500 for college expenses.

Paper Route, 1986-1988. Self-employed. Serviced a forty-customer route, five days per week. Missed only three days in two years. Collected 95 percent of debits.

EDUCATION: Graduated Commercial High School; Commerce, GA; June, 1992; Top 25 percent of class

EXTRACURRICULAR ACTIVITIES:

Debate team, two years

Student Council, senior representative

Baseball team, co-captain (short stop)

Fellowship for Christian Athletes, social chairman

Peer counselor, teen hotline

PERSONAL: Enjoy challenges and responsibility. Career goal is to be a certified financial planner and investment counselor.

- REFERENCES AVAILABLE UPON REQUEST -

9 Making the Most of Your Interview

The Top 5 Ways to Flunk Your Job Interview

(The following incidents are true stories and are listed in descending order)

5. Scoot your chair up to the interviewer's desk and begin thumbing through her in-basket.
4. Arrive 30 minutes late, and drag in 12 family members including your grandparents and children—even the maid—all of whom lobby frantically on your behalf.
3. After supper with the senior V.P., ask the waiter for a doggie bag.
2. Wear a large gold ring through your nostril.
1. Prop your feet on the interviewer's desk and ask for a Coke![1]

These true stories were gleaned from veteran corporate and executive recruiters, who considered them the worst mistakes they've seen.

Everything you have done to this point—identifying your career goals, your résumé, your phone contacts, your letters, and much more has been for one purpose: to get an interview.

Congratulations! Landing an interview is a significant step toward your new job. Your hard work, research, and résumé preparation have paid off. Don't let your exhilaration distract you from the two-fold purpose of the interview. First, the employer will be checking you out to see if you're the best qualified candidate for the job; and second, to determine if you will fit with the team.

Just as important, this is your opportunity to determine if you match the job. The interview is simply a key step toward your goal—getting a job where you use your talents for God's glory.

Preparing for the Interview

SPIRITUAL STEPS

Being scrutinized is seldom easy, so keeping the "big picture" in mind will help as you prepare for the interview. Remember who you are, and Whose you are. Nothing can change that (Romans 8:31-39), not even a poor interview.

1. Pray. Ask God for wisdom (James 1), grace, and insight, both for you and the interviewer. Since it's not automatic that you will want the job, you will need discernment.
2. If you're nervous, confess that to the Lord. Ask for His peace that passes all understanding (Philippians 4).
3. Give thanks for the way God has created you (Psalm 139).
4. Give thanks for God's work through your job search (Romans 8:28-29) and for the ways He is reshaping you to be like His Son through these circumstances.
5. Remember, you have been bought with a price (1 Corinthians 6:19-20). The value of your personhood does not rest on the affirmation from an interview.

RESEARCH STEPS

In order to be fully prepared and ready for your interview, consider the following steps.

1. Investigate the company and mission statement. Ask for company promotional materials. Check libraries for recent newspapers and periodicals. Be as familiar with company's products and services as possible. Network with employees of the company or peers in the field. You are literally "on trial," so go with as much evidence as possible.
2. Be sure you know the name of the interviewer.
3. Call the day before to confirm time of the interview, the length, location, and address.
4. If possible, make a dry run the day before. Drive to the location, see where the entrance is, and identify several areas to park. Fill the car with gas. You may even want to vacuum the car and get it washed to add to your confidence.
5. Obtain a copy of the job description if possible. Focus your preparation on how your particular background, training, and talents match you to this job. If you're not clear on this prior to the interview, it won't clear up while under the stress of the interview.

WHAT TO WEAR

"While in Rome, do as the Romans do." That saying captures the primary rule to follow when dressing for an interview. Simply dress in clothing that you typically would wear to work in the new job. For instance, there's no need to wear a three-piece European designer suit to an interview with Midas Muffler.

If possible, secure a copy of the dress code of the company. If that's not possible, dress in a conservative manner that won't distract from your mission: presenting yourself for the new job.

HINTS FOR MEN

As a general rule, the darker the suit, the more authority is implied. However, don't wear a black suit to the interview (unless it's with a mortician).

Ties should complement your suit. If you're not sure, take the suit to a men's clothing store and purchase a new tie with the assistance of the manager. Don't wear a tie with a nature scene, animals, or sporting events.

Usually a white shirt is perceived as professional and conservative. Save the loud prints for a more informal social gathering, not your interview.

HINTS FOR WOMEN

As with men, the operative word is conservative. A business suit is preferred in conservative colors such as navy blue, gray, or a charcoal.

Avoid overkill on make-up, fragrances, and jewelry.

IT GOES WITHOUT SAYING

Be sure to bathe, have your hair trimmed and presentable, use deodorant, and brush your teeth. You won't impress anyone if you're wearing lunch in your teeth. If you have a problem with recurring bad breath, take a roll of breath mints along. Fingernails should be clean.

Remember, you have one chance at a first impression. Make it good so you can focus on your real mission: presenting yourself in a positive light as the best candidate for the job opening.

WHILE YOU'RE WAITING

Plan to arrive 10-15 minutes early. You may get invited in for extra informal "chat" time. Don't overlook the receptionist who may be informally sizing you up. If you have to wait, use your eyes and ears. Learn all you can from simply studying the reception area. Relax. Focus your thoughts on greeting the interviewer. Keep your wits about you so you can engage in small talk, if it's appropriate. Do not chew gum.

Maximizing Your Interview

No matter how well planned your search has been, how professional your résumé is, or how eloquent your phone conversations were, the interview is what will get you the job offer. Do not underestimate the importance of this phase of the job search. Companies do not just interview applicants without purpose. Once you have been asked to interview, you have already successfully reached one of your goals; but the next goal—getting the job offer—requires keen preparation.

Knowing how to handle yourself and come across well in an interview is a skill. Like any skill, it is something that must be learned and practiced before you become proficient and feel confident.

FACE TO FACE WITH THE INTERVIEWER

- First impressions are very important.
- Appearance is very important.
- Give a firm handshake.
- Be yourself, confident, cheerful, frank, honest.
- Relax as the interview progresses.
- Expect some easy, relaxed questions.
- Also expect "curve" questions; listen carefully.
- Think about your answer; then speak.
- It's okay to pause on tough questions.

Interviews often fall into five phases: opening, fact-finding, information-giving, questioning period, and closing. The conversation may spill over between these phases.

PHASE 1—OPENING

- Practice your first two minutes.
- Include normal pleasantries.
- Determine the time frame for the interview.
- Be pleasant, cooperative, and very observant.
- Allow the interviewer to set the tone.
- Display focused interest, controlled energy, and a positive attitude.
- Pray inwardly during pauses (see Nehemiah 2:4).

PHASE 2—FACT FINDING

- Interviewer will explore your background, experience, and skills.
- Be positive, brief, and to the point.
- Never lie about your experience.
- Relate your experience to the company's needs.
- Show your technical/professional knowledge.
- Identify your major achievements.
- Don't go off on tangents.
- Watch for signals to stop talking.

PHASE 3—INFORMATION GIVING

- Interviewer will give information on company and job. Listen intently; taking notes is okay.
- Limit your questions at this point.
- At the right time, ask about work to be done, company goals, problems, key elements needed for success.

PHASE 4—QUESTIONING PERIOD

- Your chance to ask questions.
- Often blends with other phases.
- Focus on the job.
- Be sure you learn what the new job entails.

PHASE 5—CLOSING

- Depending on who is interviewing, seek some sort of commitment.
- Arrange some sort of follow-up if they haven't.
- Don't overstay your welcome.
- Leave an extra copy of a résumé.

TRAPS TO AVOID

• Watch out for habitual signs of nervousness—i.e., laughing, finger fidgeting, squirming, leg swinging. Everyone is nervous during an interview, but you can control the amount of nervousness you display.

• Do not be overly concerned with the possibility of a rejection. Instead, focus on the possibility of getting the job and how your experience can help this company. Every interview is a learning experience.

• *Never* be critical of a company or the performance of anyone employed there. Above all, *don't* "bad mouth" a former boss.

• Do not argue. Sell yourself with confidence, but always keep the discussion friendly and open.

• Do not *show* irritation with delays or interruptions, even if you are irritated. Help the interviewer conduct a good interview. Be courteous and considerate. Always leave yourself plenty of time for an interview.

• Do not apologize for things you cannot change or are not responsible for (your age, education, or work history).

• Do not pretend or lie.

• Do not be afraid that there is something you don't know. No one is totally knowledgeable about everything.

• Do not tell "war stories" or give long descriptions of "what happened when . . .," unless you have been encouraged to do so.

• Do not smoke, even if the interviewer indicates you may.

• Do not use expressions such as "like" and "you know." Avoid too many "ers" and "uhs." Take your time and think *before* you speak.

• Do not be in a rush to answer every question immediately; not all questions have simple, easy answers. Interviewers tend to be suspicious (and rightly so) of glib, simplistic solutions.

• Do not underestimate the influence of a receptionist, personnel department employee, or some other non-decision maker. They often have input and could make or break your chances. He or she should be viewed with respect, not as unimportant.

Typical Interview Questions

Having a good understanding of how you are going to answer specific questions is crucial to presenting your unique background, knowledge, skills, and abilities to a prospective employer.

Shown below are some "hypothetical," often-asked interview questions for your review and for which you need to prepare written answers. Writing your answers will allow you to formulate your thoughts and ideas. It also will provide a quick and easy way to review and refresh your memory prior to your interviews. Study each question *before* you start jotting down your answers, and do not underestimate its potential difficulty.

• **What were your duties, responsibilities, and accomplishments in your last job?** (Be specific and show that you know what you are talking about. If your last job was not related to the job for which you are interviewing, answer based on your most recent job that does apply.)

• **Briefly describe your educational background.** (Answer all questions the way they are asked—when an interviewer says *briefly*, that is what is meant.)

• **Would you briefly summarize your work history?** (Again, answer the question—be specific, but not wordy.)

• **Why are you leaving your current job?** or **Why are you interested in a new position at this time?** (Give an answer that does not reflect negatively on you, the company, or other individuals.)

• **Tell me about yourself.** or **Give me a thumbnail sketch of yourself.** (Have a concise response ready. Exactly what you say is not usually as important as providing a clear, orderly, and logical response. Avoid rambling and needless detail.)

• **What are your career goals?** (Phrase your response in a way the potential employer can relate to.)

• **What do you consider your major assets?** or **What are your strengths?** (This is not a time for you to be overly modest. Present your assets with assurance.)

• **Do you have any weak points?** or **What are your weaknesses?** (Everybody has some, but indicate only something that has positive implications. For example, "Because I want to see a job done correctly, I tend to be somewhat of a perfectionist.")

• **To what do you most attribute your success (failures)?** (This could be one or two questions. It deals with values and attitude. Your strategy for this question is to be both candid and positive. You should deal mainly with success, but if you must discuss a recent failure or disappointment, like losing your job, emphasize what you have learned as a result. Remember, *do not* "bad mouth" your previous employers.)

• **What represents success to you?** (This question directly asks you to express your values. It is essential not to try to answer this question based on what you think the prospective employer wants to hear, but you must answer what is in your heart. You may fool the interviewer, but you will not fool yourself. Not answering honestly, on this or any question, may mean you will get a job where you will be miserable.)

• **What was your biggest accomplishment at your most recent job?** (Tell what you have actually accomplished, not merely the tasks you have performed.)

• **What do you tend to do outside of work?** (Give a rounded and balanced picture of yourself, but be honest.)

• **Is there anything else you would like to say about yourself with regard to this job?** (You may answer this question somewhat differently at each interview, but you should have an overall strategy for your answers. In most instances, this question is your opportunity to summarize and to sell yourself.)

After the Interview, Follow Up Your Contacts

Be diligent in following up every contact, every lead, and every interview.

Timely follow-up shows you are motivated, professional, and you really appreciate the interest and assistance of others. Follow-up also allows others another opportunity to get to know you. Follow-up may be done in several ways:

• Personal note;

• Personal note and résumé, or printed 3" x 5" card with your qualifications (résumé highlights); or

• Telephone call. ◆

ENDNOTES

1. "Doomed Days: The worst mistakes recruiters have ever seen," *The Wall Street Journal,* February 27, 1995, sec. R: 4.

10 Starting a Business

Many people who are unhappy in their jobs, or who are without jobs, consider going into business for themselves. Sometimes this is a good option and sometimes it's not. Starting a business can be a complex undertaking, requiring much prayer and consideration, and we could not begin to cover every aspect in this manual. However, Christian Financial Concepts has learned a lot from counseling with those who have been both successful and unsuccessful in business start-ups. In this chapter we till touch on some of the key areas and ask some questions that will help you evaluate the wisdom of starting a business.

We also know that there are many mothers who are considering starting a home business. We think that's a good way for many women to use their talents to generate some income and still stay at home with their children. Home businesses are generally for supplemental income and usually are much simpler to get going than a full-fledged business. Still, it's important for the home entrepreneurs to know what they are getting into.

Whatever your situation, working through this section will introduce you to some of the issues you'll need to consider before starting a business. Answering the questions below will help you "count the cost" before you begin the building process.

▶▶ Motivation

As in most other decisions, you should always analyze your motivation for pursuing a course of action. Proper motivation for starting a business might include a strong desire to provide a product or service or a specific talent or idea that could be marketed by you better than by someone else. Quite often people want to start a business out of frustration with their current employment situation. That may or may not be a good idea since, for most people, there are other alternatives. The following questions will help you to analyze your motivations.

a. What is your real motivation for considering self-employment? List your reasons in order of priority.

(1.) ______________________________

(2.) ______________________________

(3.) ______________________________

(4.) ______________________________

(5.) ______________________________

b. What don't you like about your current situation?

____

c. What alternatives have you considered other than self-employment?

____

d. What values and needs are not being met in your current situation?

____

e. Starting a business takes a lot of commitment and hard work. It can be a challenge of enormous magnitude, and it usually takes a burning desire to overcome the obstacles. Is this something you really want and feel strongly led to do?

____

"And whatever you do, whether in word or deed, do it all in the name of the Lord Jesus, giving thanks to God the Father through Him" (Colossians 3:17).

Knowledge/Experience

Larry Burkett often advises us to avoid getting financially involved in things we don't know anything about. That principle especially applies to starting a business, because it requires an investment of money plus time and energy.

a. What is your knowledge level about the business you would undertake?

____

b. Do you know what defines a Christian business, and have you studied God's principles for operating a business?

____

Note: If not, we recommend you read *Business by the Book* by Larry Burkett.

c. How much experience do you have in the occupational field you are considering?

____

____

d. Do you have any business experience (profit and loss responsibility)?

____

e. Have you investigated the government regulations governing the potential business? Are licenses required?

____

____

f. Are you knowledgeable of the income and Social Security tax requirements that govern self-employed individuals?

____

NOTE: This can be a shock to those who have not had to pay quarterly taxes or self-employment tax.

g. Do you know how to write a business plan? Have you written a business plan? (If not, check with the Small Business Development Center nearest you.)

____

Start-up Capital

Most businesses fail in the first two years because they are undercapitalized. Before launching into a business, you need to "count the cost" of everything you will need to succeed.

"He who works his land will have abundant food, but the one who chases fantasies will have his fill of poverty" (Proverbs 28:19).

Rather than be too optimistic, plan conservatively regarding income and liberally regarding expenses. A frequent problem is that the business does not generate adequate income to pay overhead and provide a livable income. Entrepreneurs tend to be too optimistic about how long it will take to develop a business to the point of profitability. Thus they end up living off the money that should be paying the overhead (creditors), and they sink further in debt while trying to hold on until the business takes off.

During business start-up, a common mistake is to live by using credit cards. This virtually guarantees a financial disaster and should be avoided.

a. Where will your start-up and operating capital come from? Do you have enough cash or liquid assets to operate eighteen months to two years without a profit? (That is a good planning figure for how long it will take for most businesses to become profitable.)

____

____

____

b. Are you considering forming a partnership?

____

NOTE: Experience shows that partnerships rarely work out. If you are yoked to someone and that person (or his or her spouse) has different values and motivations than you, you won't be very happy. It's similar to a marriage, except more difficult to maintain. Successful partnerships require both parties to have the mind of Christ (a servant's attitude toward the other partner.) With two or more families involved, that rarely occurs.

Financial Records

Quite often those who have an entrepreneurial bent are the very ones who don't enjoy detail work, such as record keeping.

Not having good financial records can cause major problems because a business owner must make decisions every day, based on how things are going financially. If you don't know where you stand financially, you run a high risk of acting out of ignorance and making a bad (costly) decision.

Keep in mind that the best set of financial records for you will be something you can thoroughly understand. You may have to get some help at first and do some study on your own as well, but the keys to remember are *simplicity* and *timeliness.* Having something that is simple and current is essential for sound financial management. Two such systems are listed later in the Resource Section of this chapter.

"The sluggard is wiser in his own eyes than seven men who answer discreetly" (Proverbs 26:16).

a. What plans have you made for keeping simple, timely, and accurate financial records?

____

____

____

b. Who will be the detail person in your operation? Can you do it? Will your spouse be better suited to this task? Or will you hire someone to assist you?

____

c. If you are not experienced in the use of financial records, such as income statements, balance statements, budgets, and the like, how will you become knowledgeable about these areas?

____

____

____

Counsel and Information

You'll need information from several sources, but your counsel should come from those who have wisdom that comes from a godly perspective toward everything in life. Local Christian businesspeople can be your best source of counsel.

Small Business Development Centers are located in most states and are operated through state universities. They provide help to people who are considering business start-ups, as well as to those who already have businesses. Information is usually free or provided at a very low cost.

"Listen to advice and accept instruction, and in the end you will be wise" (Proverbs 19:20).

a. Have you received adequate counsel regarding the pros and cons of owning your own business?

____

b. Have you developed a list of sources for counsel and information?

____

NOTE: Some of the books listed at the end of this chapter contain excellent resource lists.

Personnel

The simplest business by far is a one-person operation, in which the owner *is* the business. However, many situations will require additional employees. The minute you hire one person, the situation changes considerably because many laws and rules apply that complicate the workload. You need to be familiar with withholding taxes, FICA, the Fair Labor Employment Act, OSHA, Worker's Compensation, and many other areas.

Also, in any business, getting the right person is so important.

A bad hire is one of the worst things that can happen to a small business owner. Develop a job description and criteria for the job before you start looking for the person.

As you look for your personnel, keep in mind the principles you have learned about matching the person to the job in Chapters 1–4 of this manual. The same concepts apply. If you know the pattern of what it will take to do the job, then you can look for a person with that pattern when hiring. Generally, we find that an entrepreneur's first hire should be someone who is opposite from him or her. If you are a big-picture person, you will likely need a detailed person to follow through on day-to-day activities and record keeping. Conversely, if you are a detailed person, you will likely need an outgoing, enterprising person to promote the business. Go back and study the personality section in Chapter 2 as you think through the type of person you want to hire.

Consider the following questions before hiring someone.

"Now the body is not made up of one part but of many" (1 Corinthians 12:14).

a. Are you familiar with the rules and regulations that apply to employees?

____

b. Have you developed a written job description for the opening you want to fill?

____

c. Have you given consideration to the pattern of the person you want to hire?

____

Skills and Abilities ______; Vocational Interests _____;
Work Values ______; Personality ______.

Timing a Business Start-up

As in any other endeavor, timing can be of the utmost importance. Timing can apply to you in your life and situation, and it also can apply to the product and services you offer.

a. Is the endeavor compatible with your life and other responsibilities at this time? Has the window of opportunity closed, has it just opened, or will it not open until some future date?

____

b. Is the timing right for this particular product or service?

____

This is really a marketing question that will require some careful thought, advice, and research.

Personality

Generally entrepreneurs tend to operate from a confident, results-oriented, problem-solver, and challenge-oriented (Dominant) personality style. They are usually big-picture visionaries who believe they can overcome any obstacles that arise. There are, however, good examples of every personality style being effective as business leaders.

The secret is to know your strengths and weaknesses and work within them, adapting to the situation as necessary.

You should be aware, however, that any time you adapt very much for an extended period of time, stress results. If you have high needs for stability and security, you may not want to undertake the risks of being an entrepreneur.

Entrepreneurs generally must be willing to take risks; sometimes they succeed and sometimes they fail. The principle of risk versus return applies here the same as in any other investment. The higher the anticipated return, the higher the risk. You should understand your personality and give this area high priority in your decision to start a business.

Is your temperament suited to owning and operating your own business? Evaluate your strengths based on the information in "Your Pattern," the information on personality in Chapter 2, and the entrepreneur appraisal below.

"The way of a fool seems right to him, but a wise man listens to advice" (Proverbs 12:15).

ENTREPRENEUR APPRAISAL

Assess your personal potential to operate your own home-based business. Circle a number for each statement to indicate how well it describes you or how you feel. (1=not at all, 2=sometimes, 3=often, 4=usually, 5=always)

1 2 3 4 5 I like to be in charge and usually lead groups in which I work.

1 2 3 4 5 I tend to see the "whole picture" and all aspects of any project.

1 2 3 4 5 I am a leader of people; others look to me for direction.

1 2 3 4 5 I realistically assess my talents and abilities.

1 2 3 4 5 I ask for advice from experts in fields where I need help.

1 2 3 4 5 I am thorough and accurately complete tasks I begin.

1 2 3 4 5 I enjoy solving problems and see obstacles as opportunities.

1 2 3 4 5 I schedule my day and my activities and stick to my schedule.

1 2 3 4 5 Risk taking gives me a feeling of excitement.

1 2 3 4 5 I delegate work to others and remove myself from the project, accepting their processes and results.

1 2 3 4 5 I usually bounce back very quickly after a setback.

1 2 3 4 5 I am willing to devote myself to my business.

1 2 3 4 5 My attention is not easily diverted from tasks.

1 2 3 4 5 I have a planned budget that I do not exceed.

1 2 3 4 5 I don't usually buy from door-to-door or telephone solicitors.

1 2 3 4 5 I accept responsibility for the outcome of projects I undertake.

1 2 3 4 5 Disappointments and delays do not deter me from plans or goals I have set for myself.

1 2 3 4 5 I am goal-oriented and have a 1-year, 5-year, and 10-year plan.

1 2 3 4 5 I balance my checkbook every month.

1 2 3 4 5 After much prayer, I feel strongly that God is leading me in the home business direction.

Scoring: Add the circled numbers. If you scored 80 or above, you should have no problem operating your own home-based business. If you scored below 60, you may want to look at those items in which you scored the lowest and ask yourself, "What prevents me from doing those things?"

The Entrepreneur Appraisal was developed by career counselor, Valerie Acuff, and is reprinted by permission of "HomeWork: The Home Business Newsletter with a Christian Perspective," a resource for home business, PO Box 394, Dept CP, Simsbury, CT 06070.

Time - Energy - Family

A realistic evaluation of the time commitment required to start and operate a business is essential. Solving one problem after another will require energy—physical energy and emotional energy—that comes from your drive and enthusiasm to see a project completed. A business start-up can be a consuming experience, and frequently marriages and families suffer, even to the point of breakup. Consider these questions in this area.

"No servant can serve two masters. Either he will hate the one and love the other, or he will be devoted to one and despise the other. You cannot serve both God and Money" (Luke 16:13).

a. Do you understand the time commitment required to see this undertaking through successfully?

____

b. Are you a high energy person? Is your enthusiasm so high that your work will seem like play?

____

c. How will the business affect your relationship with your spouse?

____

d. How will the business affect your relationship with your children? Will you be able to spend quantity time with your family, as well as quality time?

____

e. How will your business endeavors affect your relationship with the Lord?

____

God's Will

Go back to the first section on *motivation* in this chapter. Consider your true motivations for pursuing this course of action in light of what you believe God would have you do.

a. Have you truly sought God's will in this decision?

____

b. Will this decision enable you to better glorify the Lord in your work?

____

c. Do you and your spouse both have peace in the decision that this is truly God's will for your life?

____

Conclusion

"Whatever you do, work at it with all your heart, as working for the Lord, not for men" (Colossians 3:23).

We have taken you through the above issues because they cover the "Hall of Horrors" museum of common mistakes made when starting a business. It is not intended to discourage you but to assist you in making a good decision.

Remember, every situation is different, so every issue discussed above won't apply with the same significance. If you are going to sell homemade pies to your friends and neighbors, your situation is fairly simple, but if you expand into a small baking operation employing several people, your situation will be quite different.

We can't emphasize enough the importance of prayerful and patient consideration in making a decision to start a business. Do your homework and let the Lord guide you into His will.

Resources

BOOKS

**Business by the Book*, Larry Burkett. Nashville, TN: Thomas Nelson, 1990.

**Home Business 101*, Sharon Carr. Old Tappan, NJ: Fleming H. Revell Company, 1989.

Homemade Business, Donna Partow. Colorado Springs, CO: Focus on the Family, 1992.

Contains an excellent resource section for any new business.

Working at Home, Lindsey O'Connor. Eugene, OR: Harvest House, 1990.

Contains an excellent resource section for any new business.

**Can be purchased from Christian Financial Concepts materials department, (800) 722-1976.*

NEWSLETTERS

HomeWork: The Home Business Newsletter with a Christian Perspective, PO Box 394 Dept CP, Simsbury, CT 06070

A bimonthly newsletter for people who work at home, or plan to. Written with a Christian perspective.

Money Matters; A monthly Christian economic newsletter, 601 Broad St SE, Gainesville, GA 30501

From Larry Burkett and Christian Financial Concepts.

CHRISTIAN ORGANIZATIONS SUPPORTING BUSINESS LEADERS

Christian Businessmen's Committee of the USA

1800 McCallie Ave, Chattanooga, TN 37404,
(615) 698-4444

This organization's purpose is to assist businesspeople to operate their companies according to God's principles and sharing the gospel of Jesus Christ through their businesses.

"Masters, provide your slaves with what is right and fair, because you know that you also have a master in heaven" (Colossians 4:1).

Christian Financial Concepts

601 Broad St SE, Gainesville, GA 30501, (404) 534-1000

Provides business seminars given by qualified instructors throughout the United States. A business seminar schedule is available upon request.

Fellowship of Companies for Christ

4201 North Peachtree, Suite 200, Atlanta, GA 30341,
(404) 457-9700

This is a membership organization that conducts various business seminars for its members.

Turn Around, Inc.

PO Box 697, Griffin, GA 30224, (404) 229-9119

This ministry counsels people who are facing or have already filed for bankruptcy.

RECORD KEEPING SYSTEMS

McBee Systems

299 Cherry Hill Rd, Parsippany, NJ 07054,
(201) 263-3225

This organization may be contacted for information on setting up a business bookkeeping system.

Safeguard Business Systems

455 Maryland Dr, Fort Washington, PA 19034,
(800) 523-2422

This organization may be contacted for information on setting up a business bookkeeping system.

TAPE SERIES

"God's Principles for Operating a Business," Larry Burkett. Gainesville, GA: Christian Financial Concepts, 1989, (800) 722-1976. ◆

THE ROAD OF LIFE

At first, I saw God as my observer, my judge, keeping track of the things I did wrong, so as to know whether I merited heaven or hell when I die. He was out there sort of like a president. I recognized His picture when I saw it, but I really didn't know Him.

But later on when I met Christ, it seemed as though life were rather like a bike ride, but it was a tandem bike, and I noticed that Christ was in the back helping me pedal.

I don't know just when it was that He suggested we change places, but life has not been the same since.

When I had control, I knew the way. It was rather boring, but predictable . . . It was the shortest distance between two points.

But when He took the lead, He knew delightful long cuts, up mountains, and through rocky places at breakneck speeds; it was all I could do to hang on! Even though it looked like madness, He said, "Pedal!"

I worried and was anxious and asked, "Where are you taking me?" He laughed and didn't answer, and I started to learn to trust.

I forgot my boring life and entered into the adventure. And when I'd say, "I'm scared," He'd lean back and touch my hand.

He took me to people with gifts that I needed, gifts of healing, acceptance and joy. They gave me gifts to take on my journey, my Lord's and mine.

And we were off again. He said, "Give the gifts away; they're extra baggage, too much weight." So I did, to the people we met, and I found that in giving I received, and still our burden was light.

I did not trust Him, at first, in control of my life. I thought He'd wreck it; but He knows bike secrets, knows how to make it bend to take sharp corners, knows how to jump to clear high rocks, knows how to fly to shorten scary passages.

And I am learning to shut up and pedal in the strangest places, and I'm beginning to enjoy the view and the cool breeze on my face with my delightful constant companion, Jesus Christ.

And when I'm sure I just can't do anymore, He just smiles and says . . . "Pedal."

—author unknown

(Taken from *Holy Sweat*, Tim Hansel, Dallas TX: Word Inc., 1987. Used with permission.)

11 Facing Tough Times

From time to time, we all experience adversity in our lives. In fact the older we get the more we realize that conflicts, difficulties, and hardships are a major part of life. Unfortunately, there are times when the weight of the situation seems overwhelming and we become discouraged.

This chapter was included to encourage those who are bearing a heavy weight due to difficulties with career, family, finances, or some other problem area. We hope it will help you attain a clearer perspective of your situation and provide some practical ways to overcome the discouragement and deal with the problem.

Adjust Your Perspective

When you are faced with severe difficulties, the problems come closer and closer until your perspective is out of focus. Diagram A below graphically depicts what the counselor commonly observes in a client's situation. The problem has become so great that perspective is lost.

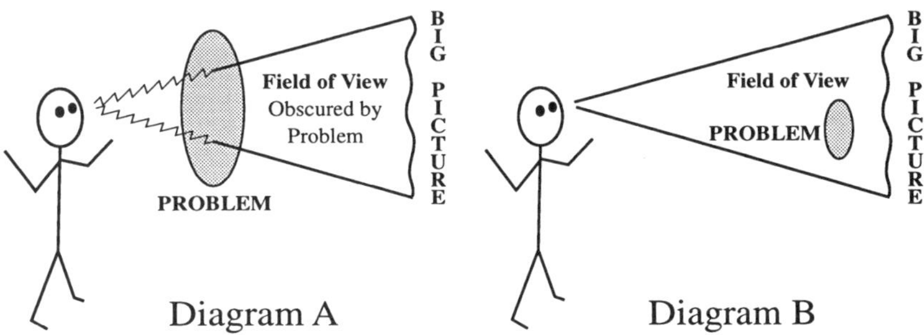

Diagram A

Diagram B

One of the first steps the counselor takes is to try to help the client move the problem back into a more realistic focus, as shown in diagram B. Somehow the client has to be able emotionally to step back and look at the situation objectively. At a distance you can see the magnitude of the problem better, compared to the big picture of life.

Look at the Examples of Others

A good technique for getting a more objective view of a problem is to focus on someone else's situation. It's usually easier to see a biblical principle in someone else's life than in our own.

Then we can compare our situation to theirs, apply the principle, and see God's grace and sovereignty at work in our lives.

Consider several examples from history to help you gain a new focus on your problem.

"I am your brother Joseph, the one you sold into Egypt! And now, do not be distressed and do not be angry with yourselves for selling me here, because it was to save lives that God sent me ahead of you" (Genesis 45:4-5).

Remember the experiences of **Joseph**, a favored child who was sold into slavery by his brothers. Taken to Egypt, he moved up to estate manager only to be falsely accused, imprisoned, and then forgotten for two years by a former cell mate he had helped. But as Joseph said to his brothers when he became prime minister of Egypt: *"It was not you who sent me here, but God"* (Genesis 45:8). Joseph saw the principle that God uses our weaknesses, our suffering, our imprisonment to glorify Him and to prepare us for greater responsibilities in His Kingdom.

Next, think about **Moses**, a man who had been groomed to be a leader of his country, yet he found himself an outcast sitting by a well in the desert. Moses went from the king's court to unemployment, then to 40 years of service in the lowest job in society. All this was in preparation to fulfill his calling as a leader of God's people and the architect of God's law.

Twelve hundred years later, we see the apostle **Paul**, probably the most brilliant mind of his time, sitting in jail. Talk about an unfair situation, hard times, depravity! What a comedown for a man of his intellect and potential! Paul experienced it all. But, he is a great role model for us because he understood hard times. His comments are instructive to us. *"But he said to me, 'My grace is sufficient for you, for my power is made perfect in weakness.' . . . That is why, for Christ's sake, I delight in weaknesses, in insults, in hardships, in persecutions, in difficulties. For when I am weak, then I am strong"* (2 Corinthians 12:9-10).

"No discipline seems pleasant at the time, but painful. Later on, however, it produces a harvest of righteousness and peace for those who have been trained by it" (Hebrews 12:11).

During my own experiences as **a prisoner of war** for five and one-half years in North Vietnam, I remembered Paul's words. I had only two meals a day of pumpkin soup and rice or bread, no television, magazines, or any of todays "necessities," and no mail for years. In fact, I could carry everything I owned under one arm. Threats, torture, and constant negative propaganda were a way of life in the POW camp. Still, I had peace of mind. I was able somehow to trust that God would use that experience to His honor and glory. My suffering had a purpose. I made it through that experience—not because of my own strength but because of God's faithfulness. I was held up by His everlasting arms and the prayers of thousands back home.

It is usually through our suffering that we learn the true lessons of faith. When everything is going our way, we tend to rely on ourselves. But when suffering brings us to the "end of ourselves," it is quite amazing how we begin to see our weaknesses—our fallibility. Confronted with our own inadequacies, we begin to relinquish control and trust in our Lord and King. And it is through hardship that we usually come to know the power of our Savior and the spiritual principles He wants us to live by. He often uses us in our weaknesses, rather than our achievements, to further His Kingdom.

"This is what the Lord says: 'Let not the wise man boast of his wisdom or the strong man boast of his strength or the rich man boast of his riches, but let him who boasts boast about this: that he understands and knows me, that I am the Lord, who exercises kindness, justice and righteousness on earth for in these I delight,' declares the Lord" (Jeremiah 9:23-24).

These examples emphasize the point that even in tough times it is our faith, our conviction, and our attitude that make the difference. If we really believe that God is who He says He is, then our job is to serve wherever we are. At times we suffer; at times we prosper; but, at all times, let us live so that others will see Jesus in us.

In whatever state we are in, we can be encouraged because we know that God is in control, and He has a plan for our lives.

If you are feeling the pinch right now, hang in there. Remember, God has placed you on this earth for a purpose. In the broadest sense, your purpose is to glorify Him, and this includes even the details and quality of your work. I believe your role is to honor Him by your attitude while waiting, preparing, or even suffering.

Practical Helps

STUDY GOD'S WORD REGULARLY

"Consequently, faith comes from hearing the message and the message is heard through the word of Christ" (Romans 10:17).

Jesus is both the Word and the Bread of Life. To be spiritually strong, you need daily nourishment from the Word. His Word reminds us of God's great love for us, it shows us truth, and it teaches us the principles that exemplify a godly character. As we feast on His Word, we come to know Jesus as the Way, the Truth, and the Life. As He comes to live in us, we see our burdens start to lift, and we feel the comfort of His everlasting arms.

PRAY AND MEDITATE

As we come to know the mind of God, we are able to pray in His will. Praying in His will is a powerful tool that He has directed us to use in life and labor. As we meditate on His Word and His will, the Holy Spirit (Counselor, Messenger, and Comforter) comes to us with encouragement and enlightenment.

SEEK GODLY COUNSEL

This has been covered earlier but bears repeating here. Godly counsel can come from a spouse, parent, friend, pastor, deacon, elder, prayer partner, or a Christian counselor. Sharing your burden with someone else who is holding God's hand is very important.

GET INVOLVED WITH THE BODY OF CHRIST

The responsibilities of the body of believers include bearing one another's burdens and sharing fellowship and love during difficult times. Whether your needs are emotional, financial, spiritual, or physical, you need to let others in your church know about your needs. If you are not in a church, find one, and join the Body of Christ.

READ ENCOURAGING BOOKS

Proverbs 12:25 states, *"An anxious heart weighs a man down, but a kind word cheers him up."* When facing discouragement, "borrow" from the faith and strength of others by reading uplifting Christian books. Browse through your church library or local Christian bookstore for books that speak to the particular issues you're encountering.

MAKE A PLAN AND START FOLLOWING IT

Your role is to do the process; God will take care of the results. Go back and look at the diagram on page 36 and think about your "process."

AVOID BITTERNESS

It takes only the slightest amount of bitterness to ruin your attitude and undercut your joy. Others will pick up on your attitude and begin to avoid you. Ultimately you have no credibility as a witness if you are driven by bitterness. If you are feeling bitter, you need to identify the root cause. Don't point the finger at others; they don't control your attitude.

"I consider that our present sufferings are not worth comparing with the glory that will be revealed in us" (Romans 8:18).

LOOK FOR WAYS GOD CAN USE YOUR ADVERSITY TO HIS GLORY

If you want to follow the model of Christ, you must also be willing to suffer to carry out God's plan for your life. If you are feeling unjustly persecuted, think how Jesus felt. Even though totally innocent, He was falsely accused, convicted in a trial that did not follow established legal procedures, and crucified in an agonizing and humiliating way.

Yet, it was through His suffering that we were blessed. Ask yourself, "How will God use my suffering to be a blessing to others?"

WASH SOMEONE'S FEET

Look around in your community and find those who are hurting worse than you are. Go to their aid; be a servant to them as Jesus was when He washed the feet of the disciples. In doing so you will gain a new perspective on your situation, and you'll begin to see God's grace at work in your life. See how He can use your hardships to prepare you for further work in His kingdom.

"Now that I, your Lord and Teacher have washed your feet, you should also wash one another's feet" (John 13:14).

When we claim our "rights" or "justice," we know some area of sin is having its way. When we surrender control of our lives to Christ, we give up our rights and become servants. If Christ lives in us, we are not concerned about our honor or our rights. We know that when we honor Him, He takes care of us through His love and grace, which far surpasses our understanding.

ACKNOWLEDGE THE LOVE OF GOD

Can you imagine how good you might feel about yourself if the president of the United States called you personally and said "You are a very important person to me and my administration. I am very interested in your future and I'd like to help you." Naturally, having the commander-in-chief of the most powerful country in the world take a special interest in you would tend to make you feel pretty good about yourself. But even that would not last, and eventually you'd have to look elsewhere for a way to sustain your value and importance.

"The Lord your God will himself cross over ahead of you. . . . Be strong and courageous. Do not be afraid or terrified . . . for the Lord your God goes with you; he will never leave you nor forsake you" (Deuteronomy 31:3, 6).

When we realize how much God really loves us, we have a legitimate and lasting source for our self-esteem.

We have been singled out by the Creator of the universe, the one true God, to be His covenant partner. Stop and think for a minute what that means. The most important person in the world has your best interest at heart. He wants to help you in your journey through life, and He has provided for you a Savior, an Advocate, a Counselor, and every spiritual blessing. How can we look down for long, when we have such a wonderful Friend who is ready to lift us up.

It is in times like these we would do well to read again that short, four-page letter written by Paul to the Philippians. It can be summed up in a selection of verses from Chapter 3:

"Finally, my brothers, rejoice in the Lord! It is no trouble for me to write the same things to you again, and it is a safeguard for

you. . . . I want to know Christ and the power of his resurrection and the fellowship of sharing in his sufferings, becoming like him in his death. . . . Not that I have already obtained all this, or have already been made perfect, but I press on to take hold of that for which Christ Jesus took hold of me. . . . But one thing I do: Forgetting what is behind and straining toward what is ahead, I press on toward the goal to win the prize for which God has called me heavenward in Christ Jesus" (Philippians 3:1, 10, 12, 13).

Step back from your trials and adjust your focus. Rejoice in God's great mercy and love and His ability to use your suffering for His glory. Then, press on, using the talents God has given you. Let His Holy Spirit guide you in your journey. He has already prepared the destination. ◆

12 Establishing a Budget

A Sound Financial Plan Is Essential for Good Career Planning

Finances will be a critical factor in your career planning. A good financial plan will allow you to make career choices based on biblical principles, rather than just the need for a paycheck.

Many people today are not able to pursue a career that God called them to because they are locked into repayment schedules that can be met only with a certain income. Many others could have much more career flexibility if they had managed their money and paid off their bills.

Sound financial planning is integral to sound career planning.

"And anyone who does not take his cross and follow is not worthy of me. Whoever finds his life will lose it, and whoever loses his life for my sake will find it" (Matthew 10:38-39).

Unless you are able to control your spending and live within your means, your career decisions will always be driven by the need for more money.

For example, though your heart's desire and your God-given talents may be to lead and teach young men at the YMCA, you may feel pressured to be a stockbroker in order to make more money to pay your bills.

Larry Burkett and Christian Financial Concepts have been teaching the concept of stewardship since 1976. Based on that experience, we know that most Christians struggle with finances. It seems that Jesus anticipated the depth of faith needed to surrender control of our finances to Him, because He taught about money and possessions more than anything else. Although financial management can be a struggle, at Christian Financial Concepts and Career Pathways, we see many testimonies each month describing how people became debt free and achieved the blessings of financial freedom by living on a budget.

By first recognizing that "our" money and possessions are really the Lord's and then becoming good managers for Him, we become truly free to follow His calling.

We have listed below a number of materials available from Christian Financial Concepts that can help you.

Cash Organizer

This envelope budgeting system will simplify your budgeting process by keeping you in control as you track your cash expenditures. Twelve envelopes bound in a durable navy blue cover (with six extra envelopes) neatly divide your cash among budget categories. This is the easiest way to begin a controlled spending plan—so critical during a period of career transition.

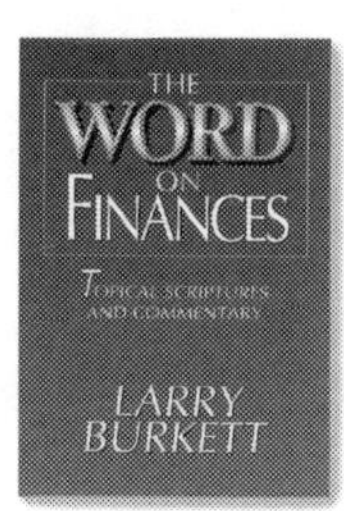

The Word on Finances

Now you can have the Bible references on money at your fingertips. All the relevant Scriptures on finances have been compiled in this easy-to-reference volume. Larry discusses more than 70 topics under the following eight comprehensive headings: right attitudes, wrong attitudes, crediting, giving and providing, God's blessings/curses, investing, work and wages, and government.

Debt-Free Living

Learn the biblical principles for getting out of debt as you follow true-to-life examples of those who sought God's sovereign direction. In this book Larry warns about certain kinds of credit and discusses alternative methods. He also addresses home ownership versus renting, the consequences of bankruptcy, common errors that lead to debt, and going from a two- to a one-income family.

The Financial Planning Organizer

The complete edition of this notebook system includes the Financial Planning Workbook, *"The Financial Planning Workshop"* audio tapes, and the *CFC Will Kit.* The workbook has easy-to-follow worksheets and step-by-step instructions that allow you to structure and maintain your budget.

Business By the Book

This book will help you discover how to build a business that will glorify the Lord and nurture employees. You'll be surprised to find out just how much God has to say about private business in His Word. A convenient study guide, included in the book, is perfect for individual or group study.

13 Striving for Contentment

. . . thoughts from Larry's desk

"But godliness with contentment is great gain" (1 Timothy 6:6).

One of the great mysteries of Christianity is contentment. At least one must presume it is a mystery, because so few people have found it. Actually, contentment is an attitude.

▶ STUDYING THE EXTREMES

On the one hand, there are many people who have seemingly little or no regard for material possessions. They accept poverty as a normal living condition, and their major concern is in which doorway to sleep. Are they living lives of contentment? Hardly so, because that description aptly fits the winos found in the bowery of New York.

In contrast are the affluent who have the best our society has to offer at their disposal. Their homes are the community showplaces, their summer "cottages" are actually small hotels, and their automobiles cost more than most families' houses. Does their abundance guarantee contentment? From observing millionaire businesspeople, star athletes, and entertainers, it's hard to imagine this group is any more "content" than the previous one.

▶ THE SECRET OF CONTENTMENT

If money can't buy it and poverty doesn't provide it, what is contentment? Contentment, contrary to popular opinion, is *not* being satisfied where you are. ***It is knowing God's plan for your life, having the conviction to live it, and believing that God's peace is greater than the world's problems.***

▶ THE ENEMIES OF CONTENTMENT

Christians get trapped into discontented lives by adopting worldly goals. These goals always boil down to more . . . bigger . . . better. Scripture defines them as indulgence, greed, and pride. Often successful people come to the Lord out of desperation when they realize that their lives are characterized by fear and anxiety. The accumulation of assets has not alleviated the fear.

Regardless of the amount of your material possessions, or lack thereof, you can have an attitude of contentment. Knowing God's plan for your life and having the conviction to live it will open the doors for contentment. Pursue contentment as a priority in your career planning.◆